At Issue

How Does Advertising Impact Teen Behavior?

Other Books in the At Issue Series:

At Issue

How Does Advertising Impact Teen Behavior?

Roman Espejo, Book Editor

GREENHAVEN PRESS
A part of Gale, Cengage Learning

GALE
CENGAGE Learning·

Detroit • New York • San Francisco • New Haven, Conn • Waterville, Maine • London

Elizabeth Des Chenes, *Managing Editor*

© 2012 Greenhaven Press, a part of Gale, Cengage Learning.

Gale and Greenhaven Press are registered trademarks used herein under license.

For more information, contact:
Greenhaven Press
27500 Drake Rd.
Farmington Hills, MI 48331-3535
Or you can visit our Internet site at gale.cengage.com

For product information and technology assistance, contact us at

Gale Customer Support, 1-800-877-4253
For permission to use material from this text or product, submit all requests online at www.cengage.com/permissions

Further permissions questions can be e-mailed to permissionrequest@cengage.com

Articles in Greenhaven Press anthologies are often edited for length to meet page requirements. In addition, original titles of these works are changed to clearly present the main thesis and to explicitly indicate the author's opinion. Every effort is made to ensure that Greenhaven Press accurately reflects the original intent of the authors. Every effort has been made to trace the owners of copyrighted material.

Cover image © Images.com/Corbis.

LIBRARY OF CONGRESS CATALOGING-IN-PUBLICATION DATA

How does advertising impact teen behavior? / Roman Espejo, book editor.
    p. cm. -- (At issue)
    Includes bibliographical references and index.
    ISBN 978-0-7377-5578-7 (hbk. : alk. paper) -- ISBN 978-0-7377-5579-4 (pbk. : alk. paper)
    1. Mass media and teenagers. 2. Advertising. 3. Teenagers--Attitudes. 4. Behavioral assessment of teenagers. I. Espejo, Roman, 1977-
    HQ799.2.M35H69 2012
    659.10835--dc23
                                                            2011026395

Printed in the United States of America
1 2 3 4 5 6 7 15 14 13 12 11

Contents

Introduction

In 2010, market research firm Keller Fay Group released a study in its TalkTrack program investigating how much teens talk about brands. The study showed that 78 percent of teens have one conversation or more about brands in media and entertainment each day, compared to 57 percent of the general population. In addition, more than half of teens discuss brands in food, beverages, retail, technology, telecommunications, and sports once or more daily. The most popular brands include Coca-Cola, Apple, McDonald's, Ford, Nike, and Hollister. "It provides clear evidence that teens need to be thought about as a distinct target, with tremendous opportunities for word-of-mouth marketing,"[1] chief executive officer Ed Keller stated about TalkTrack in 2007. "It also reinforces the need for brand and marketing managers to better understand what teens are saying about their ads and promotions," he suggested, "and to find ways to create marketing messages that resonate with teens to maximize the likelihood they will find their way into these conversations."

Some critics believe that youths' engagement with brands—by the design of advertisers and corporations—has gone too far. "One strategy marketers use is 'identity branding.' This is an explicit effort to get teens to identify themselves with a particular product or corporate brand,"[2] comments Wendell Loewen, an associate professor and pastor at Tabor College. "There is a way in which we are united by what we are being sold," he continues. "When it comes to the question, 'How do I fit?' adolescents seem to find their sense of belonging in the brand itself." Allen Kanner, child psychologist and

1. PR Newswire, "What Brands Are Teens Talking About? New TalkTrack® Survey Reveals Word of Mouth Winners," kellerfay.com, August 9, 2007.
2. *Beyond Me: Grounding Youth Ministry in God's Story*. Scottdale, PA: Faith & Life Resources, 2008.

coeditor of *Psychology and Consumer Culture: The Struggle for a Good Life in a Materialistic World*, reiterates this concern: "Teens want to identify with their peer group and in a certain sense, that is a vulnerability."[3] Kanner insists that marketers exploit this desire and associate brands with self-worth in advertisements and commercials. "More naturally, you might develop your identity around, for example, doing good in the world or building a career out of an interest," he maintains. And Alissa Quart, author of *Branded: The Buying and Selling of Teenagers*, contends that brand conscientiousness causes anxiety in young people and traps them in a cycle of conspicuous consumption. "Teens suffer more than any other sector of society for this wall-to-wall selling. They are at least as anxious as their parents about having enough money and maintaining their social class, a fear that they have been taught is best allayed by *more* branded gear,"[4] Quart argues. "And they have taken to branding themselves, believing that the only way to participate in the world is to turn oneself into a corporate product or corporate spy to help promote products to other kids."

Other researchers, however, suggest that teens are not as susceptible to branding. The Teens + Brands study conducted by TeenNick (formerly the N Channel) found conflicting attitudes among youths about brands. For instance, 29 percent of respondents agreed that "having cool brands makes me feel cool." But more than half decided that brands "are created by marketers just to get more money" and a third concurred that "if there were no brands, the world would be better." Also, in a survey by Pangea Media, 64 percent of teens claimed that clothing with brand logos is not better than unbranded clothing. Respondents made statements such as "I don't care what

---

3. "Driving Teen Egos—and Buying—Through 'Branding,'" *Monitor on Psychology*, Vol. 35, No. 6, June 2004. www.apa.org.
4. *Branded: The Buying and Selling of Teenagers*. Cambridge, MA: Perseus Publishing, 2003.

brand I'm wearing as long as I think it looks good"[5] and "I wear what I think is cool but I am kind of influenced by others." Some commentators even declare that teenagers today are savvier and more informed than ever. "Only 25 percent of teens are considered passive consumers,"[6] claims Rebecca Weeks Watson, director of development at Real Girls Media, a digital network. "This generation is opinionated and takes action," she adds. "They have been trained as shoppers since their early childhood and influence billions of dollars in spending."

To advertisers, researchers, and advocates alike, adolescents represent a unique category of consumers, characterized by greater needs for independence and choice, but lacking the psychological maturity and privileges of adults. From the advent of social media campaigns to the influence of fast food ads on eating habits, the authors in *At Issue: How Does Advertising Impact Teen Behavior?* debate the ways marketing shapes the lives of youths.

5. Seth Lieberman, "Brands Are Part Of Their Identity (Except When They're Not)," *Pangea Media*, August 6, 2009. www.pangeamedia.com.
6. "Teens: Making or Breaking Brands?" *iMediaConnection*, October 28, 2004. www.imediaconnection.com.

1

Advertising Promotes Consumerism in Children and Teens

Victor C. Strasburger, Barbara J. Wilson, and Amy B. Jordan

Victor C. Strasburger is chief of the Division of Adolescent Medicine and professor at the University of New Mexico School of Medicine. Barbara J. Wilson is vice provost for student affairs and professor at the Department for Communication at the University of Illinois at Urbana-Champaign. Amy B. Jordan is director of the Media and the Developing Child sector of the Annenberg Public Policy Center of the University of Pennsylvania.

Exposure to advertising encourages consumer desires and values in youths. For instance, several studies show that children who are heavy viewers of television want more advertised toys and consume more advertised food; their desires for such products are also increased. Furthermore, advertising creates conflicts within families when children and teens attempt to influence what parents buy. In addition to creating demand for certain items and brands, advertising may foster youths' materialistic attitudes, equating happiness with money, possessions, and the ability to buy expensive things. For adolescents, preoccupations with physical appearances and unrealistic body images may be of concern.

Asking whether advertising creates a desire for products may seem like a ridiculous question to some. American children wear T-shirts emblazoned with Pokémon characters, carry lunch boxes decorated with Disney images, wear designer jeans and Nike athletic shoes, and love anything with the word *Abercrombie* on it. Adolescents seem even more conscious of brand names as well as the latest fads in clothing and technology. Where does all this consumer desire come from? When asked, most children report that they bought something because "you see it a lot" or "everybody has one". As noted above, advertising often conveys the idea that a product will bring fun and happiness to a youngster's life. Images of other children playing with a toy or eating at a fast-food restaurant reinforce the notion that everyone else is doing it too.

Advertising and Product Desires

But does exposure to advertising create desires? A number of surveys show that children who watch a lot of television want more advertised toys and actually consume more advertised foods than do children with lighter TV habits. As an example, one recent study asked 250 children in the Netherlands to list their Christmas wishes and then compared them with the commercials that were aired on TV at the time. More than half the children requested at least one advertised product. Moreover, heavy exposure to television significantly predicted requests for more advertised products, even after controlling for age and gender of the child. Another recent study of more than 900 fifth and sixth graders found that those who watched a great deal of television had more positive attitudes toward junk food, such a sugared cereals and fast-food items, than did light viewers. Heavy TV viewers also perceived that other children ate junk food more often, and they perceived junk food to be healthier and reportedly ate more junk food themselves. These patterns held up even after controlling for gender, grade level, and socioeconomic status of the family.

Among adolescents too, exposure to television has been linked to increased desire for products and brand names.

However, evidence suggests that the strength of this relationship may decrease somewhat with age, consistent with children's growing awareness of the purpose of advertising as well as increased skepticism about such messages.

In a study of older children, exposure to a single ad or acne cream caused fourth and fifth graders to worry more about skin blemishes and to want to buy the cream.

Clearly, correlational evidence reveals that there is a relationship between TV advertising and product desires, but it is difficult to establish causality in such studies. It is possible that youth who are eager to buy toys, games, clothes, and snacks actually seek out television more often to find out about new products, a reverse direction in this relationship. Thus, researchers have turned to experiments to more firmly establish the impact of advertising.

In the typical experiment, children are randomly assigned to either view or not view an advertisement for a particular product. Afterward, children are allowed to select the advertised product from a range of other choices, or they are asked a series of questions about how much they like or want that product compared to others. Experiments generally show that commercials are indeed effective. In one study, preschoolers exposed to a single ad for a toy were more likely than those not exposed to (a) choose the toy over the favorite activity at the school, (b) select the toy even if it meant playing with a "not so nice boy," and (c) choose the toy despite their mother's preference for a different toy. In a study of older children, exposure to a single ad for acne cream caused fourth and fifth graders to worry more about skin blemishes and to want to buy the cream.

Although one ad can increase desire for a product, multiple exposures may be even more influential. [Researchers G.J.] Gorn and [M.E.] Goldberg found that viewing one versus three commercials was equally effective in increasing positive attitudes toward a new toy compared to a no-exposure control group, but only the three-exposure condition made children try harder to win the toy. Other research supports the idea that a single ad can increase awareness and liking of a product, but multiple exposures to varied commercials are most effective in changing consumer behavior.

Beyond repetition, there are other ways to enhance the impact of an advertisement. One tactic is to include a premium or prize with the product, as is done in boxes of cereal. In 1975, premiums were offered in nearly 50% of cereal ads targeted to children. This practice is less common today in cereal ads, but fast-food commercials routinely entice children with small toys that come with kids' meals. In 1997, McDonald's had difficulty keeping Teenie Beanie Babies in stock once it began offering them as premiums in kids' Happy Meals. Research suggests that premiums in commercials can significantly increase children's desire for a product and actually can affect children's requests for cereals in a supermarket.

Another strategy involves the use of a celebrity or a popular character to endorse a product in an ad. Professional athlete Michael Jordan has long been associated with Nike and even has a pair of athletic shoes (Air Jordans) named after him. There are countless other examples. Teen pop star Hilary Duff has her own Barbie doll and used to endorse Candie's fashions through Kohl's department stores. Golf star Tiger Woods is a spokesperson for American Express and pitches Macintosh computers, among other products. And [cartoon character] Bart Simpson claims to love Butterfinger candy bars.

Research supports the idea that popular figures can be effective sources of persuasion. One study found that teens perceived celebrities as more trustworthy, competent, and attractive than noncelebrity endorsers featured in nearly identical ads. Furthermore, the celebrities resulted in more favorable evaluations of a product. In a controlled experiment, [researcher R.] Ross and her colleagues exposed 8- to 14-year-old boys to a commercial for a racecar set but systematically varied whether a celebrity endorser was included in the ad. The researchers found that exposure to the celebrity significantly enhanced boys' liking of the racing set and increased their belief that the celebrity was an expert about the toy.

Taken as a whole, the research demonstrates that commercials can have quite powerful effects on children's desires. Even a single ad can change the way a child perceives a toy or a game. Ads also can persuade young viewers to eat foods that are not very nutritional and to try certain drugs such as tobacco. As it turns out, even a bland ad can make a product appealing, but incorporating tactics such as premiums and celebrity endorsers can make a pitch even more effective. Next we will consider effects of advertising that are more indirect and not necessarily intentional on the part of advertisers: increased family conflict and changes in youth values.

Parent-Child Conflict

Most advertising agency executives believe that TV commercials do not contribute to family conflict. Yet research suggests otherwise. One study presented stories to elementary schoolers about a child who sees a TV commercial for an attractive product. When asked if the child in the story would ask a parent to buy the product, nearly 60% of the children responded affirmatively. When asked what would happen if the parent said no, 33% of the children said the child in the story would feel sad, 23% said the child would be angry or hostile, and 16% said the child would persist in requesting the product. Only 23% indicated the child would be accepting of the decision.

According to mothers, children's efforts to influence purchasing occur most often for food items, especially cereals, snacks, and candy. Coincidentally, those same products are among the most heavily advertised to children. Requesting a parent to purchase something does seem to decrease with age, in part because as children get older, they have more of their own money to make independent decisions. Yet for expensive items, even adolescents can pester parents. One national survey found that 40% of 12- to 17-year-olds had asked for an advertised product they thought their parents would disapprove of, and most of these young people said they were persistent. In fact, the teens estimated that they had to ask an average of nine times before their parents gave in and made the purchase.

[A]dvertising can produce pressure on parents to buy products, which in turn can cause family conflict when such requests are denied.

Several studies actually have observed parents and children as they shop together in an effort to assess conflict more directly. In an early study, [researchers J.P. Galst and [M.A.] White observed 41 preschoolers with their mothers in a grocery store. The researchers documented an average of 15 purchase influence attempts (PIAs) by the child in a typical shopping trip, or one every 2 minutes! Most of the PIAs were for cereals and candy, and 45% of them were successful. In other words, the mother acquiesced to nearly half of the children's requests. In another observational study, Atkin found that open conflict occurred 65% of the time that a parent denied a child's request for a cereal in a supermarket.

One experiment creatively linked PIAs directly to advertising. . . . [Researchers Z.] Stoneman and [G.H.] Brody randomly assigned preschoolers to view a cartoon that contained six food commercials or no commercials at all. Immediately afterward, mothers were told to take their preschoolers to a nearby grocery store to buy a typical week's worth of groceries, purportedly as part of another study. Posing as clerks in the store, research assistants surreptitiously coded the inter-actions that occurred. Children who had been exposed to the food commercials engaged in significantly more purchase in-fluence attempts than did children in the control group. Chil-dren exposed to the commercials also made more requests for those foods that were featured in the ads. In addition, the mothers' behavior was influenced by the commercials. Moth-ers of children who had seen the ads engaged in significantly more control strategies during the shopping trip, such as put-ting the item back on the shelf and telling the child no.

In sum, advertising can produce pressure on parents to buy products, which in turn can cause family conflict when such requests are denied. Younger children who confront pa-rental resistance are likely to whine, become angry, and even cry. Older children, in contrast, tend to use more sophisticated persuasion tactics, such as negotiation and white lies. There is some evidence of gender differences in this nag factor. Boys are more forceful and demanding in their requests than girls are, and boys also tend to be less compliant. Finally, research suggests that parent-child discord is not just an American phenomenon. One cross-cultural study found that heavy tele-vision viewing among children is linked to higher parent-child conflict about purchases in Japan and Great Britain as well as in the United States.

[O]ne national poll found that 53% of teens said that buying certain products makes them feel better about themselves.

Materialism and Value Orientations

Critics worry that in addition to creating demand for certain products, advertising may contribute more generally to mate-rialistic attitudes in our youth. Materialism refers to the idea that money and possessions are important and that certain qualities such as beauty and success can be obtained from having material property. [Researcher R.F.] Fox claims that "when kids are saturated in advertising, their appetites for products are stimulated. At the same time, kids desire the values that have been associated with those products—intangible values that, like sex appeal, are impossible to buy". The popular Bratz dolls, for example, are marketed to tween girls as a "lifestyle brand" that revolves around makeup, sexualized clothing, and communal shopping and congregating at the mall. In support of this idea of materialism or hyperconsumption, one national poll found that 53% of teens said that buying certain products makes them feel better about themselves. Other critics argue that advertising should not be singled out for attack and that youthful consumerism is part of children's participation in a larger culture that has become rooted in commodities.

Disentangling advertising from all the other forces that might foster materialism is difficult, especially because nearly all children are exposed to a world filled with toy stores, fast-food restaurants, movies, peer groups, and even schools, all of which promote consumer goods. Several correlational studies have looked to see if there is a relationship between media habits and materialism in youth. To measure materialism, students are typically asked to agree or disagree with statements such as "It is really true that money can buy happiness," and "My dream in life is to be able to own expensive things." One large survey of more than 800 adolescents found that heavy exposure to television was positively correlated with buying products for social acceptance, even after controlling for age, sex, socioeconomic status, and amount of family communication about consumption. In this same study, teens who reported watching a lot of TV also were more likely to associate possessions and money with happiness. Another survey found a similar pattern for tweens. That is, 8- to 12-year-olds who frequently watched television commercials were more materialistic than were their peers who seldom watched commercials. This was true regardless of the child's age, gender, or socioeconomic status.

These patterns are certainly suggestive, but they do not permit firm causal conclusions. Materialistic youth could seek out advertising, advertising might cause materialism, or both. Clearly, longitudinal research is needed to ascertain whether heavy exposure to advertising during early childhood leads to more materialistic attitudes over time. One such study exists in the published literature. [Researchers G.P.] Moschis and [R.L.] Moore surveyed 6th through 12th graders twice, across 14 months, about their exposure to television commercials and their materialistic attitudes. At Time 1, there was a significant association between exposure to ads and materialism, as has been found in other studies. Looking over time, exposure to advertising at Time 1 also predicted higher scores on materialism 14 months later at Time 2, but *only* among those youth who were initially low in materialism. In other words, television seemed to have its greatest impact on those who were not already highly materialistic. More longitudinal research of this sort is needed, particularly with younger children whose values are still developing. Obviously, studies need to control for other relevant socialization factors, such as the parents' own values regarding material goods.

Another concern is whether advertising contributes to a preoccupation with physical appearance, especially among female adolescents. Teen magazines, in particular, are rife with ads featuring thin, attractive models. Studies have found that female adolescents and college students do compare their physical attractiveness to models featured in advertising. Moreover, looking at ads of highly attractive models can temporarily affect self-esteem and even body image, especially among girls who are encouraged to evaluate themselves. In one experiment, adolescent girls who were exposed to a heavy dose of commercials emphasizing physical appearance were more likely to believe that being beautiful is an important character-istic and is necessary to attract men than were those in a control group exposed to other types of ads. Longitudinal evidence is also beginning to emerge, suggesting that early television and magazine exposure increases young girls' desire to have a thin body and young boys' desire to have a muscular body when they grow up.

2

Peers Have the Greatest Influence on Teens' Buying Behaviors

PricewaterhouseCoopers

PricewaterhouseCoopers (PWC) is an international professional services firm headquartered in London, England.

The "friendship factor" is highly influential in shaping teens' spending habits and their tastes in music, movies, video games, and other forms of entertainment and content. Teens rely on word-of-mouth recommendations from friends and classmates who are unique and trendy "trailblazers," popular and influential, experts in certain areas, technology "geeks," and creative and engaging "storytellers." They also log on and turn to peers on social networking and content sites such as Facebook and YouTube. For advertisers and marketers, these "influencers" present an opportunity to establish brand loyalty and promote products, services, and content within these groups.

When it comes to media content, who decides what's the latest? For teens, it's their peers. The "friendship factor" can be extremely influential, with teens placing enormous value on the recommendations and tastes of their trusted friends or close-in-age family members. Teens rely on their peers to be arbiters of what's cool, what's popular—and what's not. They turn to classmates and friends as well as virtual peer groups, such as the "most popular" lists on social networking sites, like Facebook, or content sites, such as YouTube.

PricewaterhouseCoopers, "The Friendship Factor: How Teens Are Influenced About the Media and Content," *The Speed of Life: 2009 Consumer Intelligence Series*, 2009. www.pwc.com. Copyright © 2009 by Pricewaterhousecoopers Inc. Reproduced by permission.

Teens also trust the opinions of other teens they perceive as "experts"—peers who know about music, TV shows, movies, or games, and are able to fluently and creatively express their opinions. These trailblazing teens offer marketers an opportunity: those who understand the characteristics of peer influencers can tap into these groups to build brand loyalty and promote products, services or content among their peer groups.

While peers hold the most sway over teen consumers, teens are also influenced by family members, targeted advertising, or free trials or services for music and games.

Peer Influences

Who are peer influencers? These teens often have common characteristics or fall into specific groups:

Trailblazers: These influencers are viewed as leaders who are adventurous. They avidly seek new ideas, information, and trends. Many have their own sense of style. They are confident about their ability to evaluate new things and share their opinions with others.

Influencers are sometimes perceived as highly intellectual—even "geeks"—if they have a passion and expertise in specific content, particularly when it comes to games and Internet involvement.

Popular: Teens who are viewed as popular have clout and credibility. Their "coolness" comes from being admired for a collection of attributes, including confidence, intelligence, manner, good looks, and sometimes their sense of humor or athletic ability (particularly boys). The choices these influencers make are emulated by those who hold them in high esteem.

"Experts" in their field: These influencers are "in the know," often due to their immersion in one particular area, such as

music, movies, or games. They are deeply engaged or involved in the latest product introductions and innovations and viewed as experts on that particular kind of content.

Boys are more willing to change how they watch to save money: Boys say they'll watch programming on websites or download movies as a cost-saving alternative.

Geeks rule: Influencers are sometimes perceived as highly intellectual—even "geeks"—if they have a passion and expertise in specific content, particularly when it comes to games and Internet involvement: Some are even considered almost obsessive in their indulgence of a particular content. Although they may not be as popular or relatable as other influencers, their deep involvement with content enhances their reputation as an authority. Importantly, they are respected as geeks, not dismissed as freaks.

Good storytellers: These influencers share their opinions in an entertaining, creative, or artistic way, commanding the attention of their peers. This storytelling ability enhances the appeal of the content or product, and establishes these teens as an authority. Similarly, kids who are considered funny are particularly influential about humorous content.

Boys more influential than girls: Boys tend to be more influenced by their own gender about content, as their tastes are more similar than girls'. Girls, however, are influenced by both genders. Girls perceive their own gender to have an advantage in evaluating emotional content ("Boys just like action movies"), as well as female-targeted music and magazines. However, girls generally consider boys to have more expertise in video games, and to a lesser extent, humorous content.

The Power of the Internet

Networking online: Social networking applications and instant messaging play an increasingly critical—even viral—role in conveying peer influence. Particularly on Facebook, but also on MySpace and AIM [AOL Instant Messenger], influencers are able to widely publicize their favorite content by sharing music playlists; URLs to favorite videos on YouTube and other sites; and opinions about TV shows; movies: games; magazines; and other products or services.

Searching the engines: Teens also regularly use Google and other search engines to find a wide range of content and ascertain what is currently cool. Search engines are a big draw because they provide instant information about content and its popularity.

Checking the ads: Teens tend to pay attention to ads for relevant products and content—especially if the message is entertaining and engaging. Ads on television, social networks, and content-provider websites are viewed as particularly relevant vehicles.

The Influence of Brand Collaboration

What's in it for me? Teens view brand collaboration as interesting if it benefits them by making content easier to access or less expensive, as in the cooperative effort for accessing movies between Xbox Live and Netflix.

Are they talking (and listening) to me? Teens are also interested in brand collaboration when the brands are specifically relevant to them or involve products or services they might use. They also perceive the brand favorably if the collaboration allows them to express their opinions or communicate with impact, such as having the ability to communicate with an MTV host live via Twitter.

Don't force it. Teens say it is important that relationships between brands seem real and genuine. They should be intuitive and organic to the product/service, especially for the younger segment. Trying too hard is often transparent and can serve to thwart the effort entirely ("trying to be all cool makes them less cool").

The Influence of the Economic Downturn

Doing the same, just less of it: The economic downturn effects teens. Most teens in our focus groups said their families were cutting back, resulting in less disposable income for them. Meanwhile, teens generally perceive price increases on many products and services, including media and content. Although the economy has not caused teens to significantly change their media consumption habits, they have cut back on pricier items, such as game upgrades and DVD purchases. Instead, they opt for more rentals and on-demand purchases. Some are also going to the movies less frequently.

Less is more, free is better: The economic pinch has prompted teens to be more resourceful and pursue ways to get the same services, products, or content for less or for free. Many have switched from using iTunes (perceived as too expensive) to Limewire and other lower-cost or free sites for content acquisition. Although many of the sites teens turn to for low-cost or free content acquisition involve pirated content, teens perceive this as a common, widespread practice and justify their usage as a money-saving strategy. Piracy is not always equated with theft and is often rationalized as insignificant because "everyone does it," and because of the relatively low cost involved in downloading content . . . ("It's only $1.00 . . . it's not like getting free Xboxes or TVs"). Teens are willing to accept advertising in scenarios where they can get content for free, such as on music and gaming sites or free video streaming sites such as Hulu or YouTube.

> *[O]pinions are freely shared and considered critically important in determining what is popular and deserves their interest.*

Teens love trials: Free trials that offer a complimentary service or free content are extremely attractive to teens. Trials are frequently the way teens first experience new content before they commit to a purchase. Free trials are perceived as a big benefit, especially at a time when they have to be more discerning because of less disposable income.

Implications for Businesses

1. *Influential teens can be targeted and leveraged to promote content effectively among their peer groups.* Brand affinity is strong among teens; opinions are freely shared and considered critically important in determining what is popular and deserves their interest. Marketers who understand the characteristics of peer influencers can tap into these groups to win their loyalty and, in turn, boost support for services, products and content.

2. *Advertising is still a relevant and credible source of information.* This is particularly true if advertisers are visible across multiple online media platforms—such as social networks, content portals, and search engines—and can capitalize on the Internet's advanced capabilities for targeting and tracking.

3. *Brand collaboration must have a clear benefit to be valued by teens.* If savings or efficiencies are not clearly involved, brand collaboration risks being ignored.

4. *Free trials and other incentives are powerful ways to attract teen attention.* This is particularly true in light of the economic downturn, when fewer discretionary dollars trickle down from parents to teens.

5. *Content price increases to offset the elimination of copy-protection strategies can backfire in today's environment of increased price sensitivity.* This can accelerate the rate at which teens switch from paid content to "free" sites.

3

Tweens Have Become More Aware of Advertising and Brands

Jayne O'Donnell

Jayne O'Donnell is the retail reporter for USA Today *and author of* Gen BuY: How Tweens, Teens, and Twenty-Somethings Are Revolutionizing Retail.

Children as young as eight outgrow toys and children's clothing as they encounter outside influences such as the media and Internet earlier in life. Observing "kids getting older younger," marketers target tweens, or preteens, for products once considered only for teenagers. Tween girls' tastes and purchases are shaped by several factors: the desire to imitate their peers, collect a wide range of a single product, gain attention, and aspire to be like older girls and their mothers. Brands and advertisers not only cater to these traits, but aim to hook kids and groom brand loyalty as soon as possible.

Jill Brown almost cried the day her 9-year-old daughter sold several American Girl dolls at a yard sale so she could buy a Juicy Couture sweat suit.

It was a painful reminder that the emotional and psychological distance between childhood and the teen years is far shorter than ever.

"It was such an indication of her moving to a different place," says Brown, a marketing consultant in Northbrook, Ill. "It was also a little bit of an indication that she was starting to solve things for herself."

Chalk it up to "age compression," which many marketers call "kids getting older younger" or KGOY. Retail consultant Ken Nisch says it shouldn't be a surprise or an outrage that kids are tired of toys and kid clothes by 8, considering that they are exposed to outside influences so much earlier. They are in preschool at 3 and on computers at 6.

With their keen but shifting senses of style, tween girls present some of the biggest rewards and challenges for retailers and brands.

That's why marketers now target 9-year-olds with apparel and accessories once considered only for teens, says Nisch, chairman of the retail consulting and design firm JGA.

Generation Y, those between about 8 and 26, are considered the most important generation for retailers and marketers because of their spending power and the influence they have over what their parents buy. But just as the 8- to 12-year-old "tweens" are pitched with a dizzying array of music, movie and cellphone choices, the nearly 10 million tween girls also are getting more attention from fashion, skin care and makeup businesses. Last year [in 2006], NPD Group says 7- to 14-year-old girls spent $11.5 billion on apparel, up from $10.5 billion in 2004.

With their keen but shifting senses of style, tween girls present some of the biggest rewards and challenges for retailers and brands. What's called for: a delicate marketing dance that tunes in tween girls without turning off their parents, who control both the purse strings and the car. Retailers to tween girls also must stay in close touch with the fashion pulse, because being "out" is even more painful for girls who haven't hit the teen years, say retailers and their consultants. They'll drop a brand faster than you can say Hannah Montana if the clothes become anything close to dorky.

When you're a tween retailer, you're "even more subject to peer pressure, to being in or out" than those dealing strictly with teenagers, says Nisch.

Some other tween girl traits:

They're driven by imitation. Tweens want to look like each other but be able to call looks their own, says retail consultant Laura Evans, whose clients include Reebok and Express. Retailers that offer a lot of similar apparel—layers of shirts in a variety of colors—tend to be the most popular. Hilary Bell, executive vice president for strategy for Bonne Bell, says almost every young girl is introduced to the youth-oriented cosmetic brand through her mother, aunt or older sister, "But each generation, she feels like she discovered it herself." Tween Brands, which owns the Limited Too and Justice chains, finds its customer "doesn't want to set the trend on the playground," says spokesman Robert Atkinson. In some respects, this makes the tween retailer's job easier. It can follow popular trends from the teen market.

They want more of everything. Whether it's lip balm or blue jeans, "More is more," says Nita Rollins, who heads marketing intelligence at the digital marketing agency Resource Interactive. "Nothing succeeds like excess." Tweens aren't aware of "social codes of restraint," says Rollins, so they see no reason why they don't need 10 American Girl dolls or several pairs of jeans or sneakers. The average number of Lip Smacker-brand lip balm and glosses owned by Bonne Bell customers is 10, but, Bell notes, "The girls who have 100 make up for the ones who don't have 10."

Therein also lies the success of the low-priced accessories store chains Claire's and Icing. Young people even have a new website, zebo.com, on which to chronicle and quantify their possessions, and millions already have.

They are environmentally aware. Tweens start to "feel the pain of everybody. They want to know if animals were hurt in making this," says Nisch, whose clients have included H&M

and Disney. They might even become vegetarians or vegans. Rollins agrees: "They have social consciousness at a very young age. They have great lives, and so they want to give back."

Our customer aspires to be like an older girl, so if she's 10 she wants to dress like a 12-year-old, and a 12-year-old wants to dress like a 14-year-old . . .

Bonne Bell doesn't test on animals, and Hilary Bell says the company often gets e-mails from girls thanking it. The company also uses recycled paper, cardboard and plastics in packaging where possible. The girls, for the most part, "have a caring, sharing and compassionate attitude. The Earth, plants and animals are their friends," Bell says.

They like attention, sort of. "Our customer aspires to be like an older girl, so if she's 10 she wants to dress like a 12-year-old, and a 12-year-old wants to dress like a 14-year-old," says Atkinson. But she's also "more self-conscious" and not usually trying to attract boys, he says. She mostly just wants to appear "more affiliated with her friends."

Looking for Attention

Consumer psychologist Kit Yarrow says "sexy is the ubiquitous look for the entire generation, but for tweens and teens, it's not so much sexual as attention-getting." The attention more adventurous tweens get when they wear "sexy" stuff makes them feel powerful. "They just don't compute sexy the way adults do. It's a dress-up game," says Yarrow, a marketing professor at Golden Gate University.

A tween starts to feel more comfortable with fashions when she sees them on her older sister or the babysitter, says Atkinson. Tween Brands' challenge, he says, is to "tastefully interpret them for the younger customer. She's just literally developing into a young woman. She doesn't even want to wear spaghetti straps." The girl "has to want an item because she thinks it's the coolest thing in fashion, but if we don't pass muster with Mom, that transaction is not going to be completed."

Moms, in fact, are a big influence on tween fashions, experts say. Many tweens may get some fashion cues from celebrities, but they still look first to their moms. "They still want Mom to give them the OK," Atkinson says.

What else would explain all the tweens and teens with quilted and printed cloth backpacks and purses from Vera Bradley, asks Rollins. "You can't say it's because the paisleys are particularly beautiful. It's the exposure to all the brands the parents covet."

While teens have dozens of retailers catering to them and many within each subset, from preppy to Goth to skateboard style, tween girls shop in a much more narrow range. Outside of department and mass-merchandise stores, their specialty store choices are largely limited to, well, Limited Too, Justice and Abercrombie Kids.

Despite the challenges, most brands want to hook kids as early as possible, which explains kid and tween lines from the likes of Lucky Brand Jeans, J. Crew and Juicy Couture. Bell calls her brand's lip balms "a rite of entry into makeup." Tweens are the brand's core customer, but they've developed products that appeal to kids starting at age 4 and then adapt them to teens and beyond.

Lucky simply offers its adult jeans and vintage-inspired clothes in smaller sizes, choosing not to treat kids or tweens like "little dolls," says Liz Munoz, senior vice president of merchandising and design

"Our brand is about staying young at heart and having fun and being somewhat carefree from the burdens of fashion and trends," says Munoz. "I don't necessarily want my kids to look older. I just want them to wear high-quality, beautiful things."

'Fashion Battle' with a 9-year-old

If only it were so simple, says Angelina Spencer of Naples, Fla., who has an 11-year-old daughter. Spencer says she and Ryan had their first "fashion battle" when Ryan was 9.

"I refused to buy her tight midriff exposing T-shirts that Britney Spears had made so popular, (and) my resourceful daughter resorted to knotting her T-shirts in the back to give her the look she desired," says Spencer. Spencer started a dialogue with Ryan about the appropriate fit for her clothes and what she was trying to accomplish with revealing fashion.

She says it was both eye-opening and life changing. Ryan started sketching fashions, and her mother bought her a sewing machine. Ryan's favorite stores still include Abercrombie Kids, American Eagle and Hollister, but she and her mother have reached a middle ground on what's appropriate, even if it can be challenging to find clothes that satisfy both of them.

"My views of fashion have definitely changed. I used to think that the less clothes, the better," Ryan says. "I currently don't have my stomach showing anywhere but the beach."

Angelina Spencer wishes retailers let kids have more of a role in personalizing and designing their clothes. Polo Ralph Lauren has tapped into this desire, says Evans, who leads the retail team at Resource Interactive. It offers tweens and teens the chance to monogram and handpick the color combination for the logo and garment.

It's "all about carving out their own individuality" but within a very limited range, Atkinson says of tweens.

Lindsey Brown, who turned 13 last month, made almost $1,000 at the yard sale where she sold her American Girl dolls. She banked $800 and spent $200 on the Juicy Couture sweat suit, which included a skirt, pants and a jacket.

Since then, shopping has "become all about clothes," says Jill Brown.

"A couple years ago, she liked nothing better than to go to school in the same outfit as her best friend, but now she also wants to put together something that's unique to her," says Brown. "It's almost like another beginning where they still have the desire to be a little bit like everyone else but also start to become their own person. Maybe she's beginning to do that a little bit earlier."

4

Online Advertising Aggressively Targets Children and Teens

Jeff Chester and Kathryn Montgomery

Jeff Chester is the founder and executive editor of the Center for Digital Democracy. Kathryn Montgomery is a professor at the School of Communication at American University.

Breaking from the confines of traditional advertising, digital marketing pervasively intrudes upon youths' lives, with food and beverage companies leading the way. For example, video games serve as sophisticated interactive environments to collect personal information, track the behaviors of players, and target them with personalized ads. Moreover, viral marketing has grown from spreading word-of-mouth brand awareness to tapping influential youths to plug products to their peers through social networks, instant messaging, and blogs. And "brand-generated marketing" recruits children and adolescents to create and distribute commercialized content. Overall, these promotional techniques and strategies raise concerns about the choices and well-being of young people.

With the proliferation of media in children's lives, marketing now extends far beyond the confines of television and even the Internet, into an expanding and ubiquitous digital media culture. The new "marketing ecosystem" encompasses cell phones, mobile music devices, instant messaging, videogames and virtual, three-dimensional worlds. New marketing practices in these diverse media environments are fundamentally transforming how corporations—notably including food and beverage companies—sell to young people.

The influx of brands into social networking platforms—where they now have their own "profiles" and networks of "friends"—is emblematic of the many ways in which contemporary marketing has all but obliterated the boundaries between advertising and editorial content. The unprecedented ability of digital technologies to track and profile individuals across the media landscape, and engage in "micro" or "nano" targeting, raises the twin specters of manipulation and invasion of privacy. The growing use of neuropsychological research suggests that digital marketing will increasingly be designed to foster emotional and unconscious choices, rather than reasoned, thoughtful decision making. The prospect of armies of avatars (virtual people), deployed as brand "salespersons" and programmed to react to the subtlest cues from other online inhabitants, suggests a disturbing move into uncharted territory for consumer-business relationships.

A number of these practices may be inherently exploitive and unfair, or even deceptive. For adults, they are problematic enough. For children and teens, they pose even greater risks. When used to promote certain food products, the aggregation of these new marketing tactics could worsen the childhood obesity epidemic, which is already contributing to rising rates of heart and circulatory illnesses, depression and other mental illnesses, respiratory problems, and Type II diabetes, a disease that used to strike only adults.

Mobile Marketing

Cell phones are one of the most important digital platforms for marketing to young people, enabling companies to directly target users based on previous buying history, location and other profiling data. As the practice grows, mobile users will increasingly be sent personally tailored electronic pitches, designed to trigger immediate purchases and timed to reach them when they are near particular stores and restaurants.

Database marketing has become a core strategy for companies targeting teens, and a linchpin of many digital media campaigns—not only on the Internet, but also on cell phones, video games and other new platforms.

McDonald's McFlurry mobile marketing campaign was designed to "create a compelling way to connect with the younger demographic." Six hundred McDonald's restaurants in California urged young cell phone users to text-message to a special phone number to receive an instant electronic coupon for a free McFlurry dessert. Youth were encouraged to "download free cell phone wallpaper and ring tones featuring top artists," and to email the promotional website link to their friends. Ads on buses, billboards, "wild postings" near high schools, and even skywriting airplanes promoted the "Text McFlurry 73260" message.

The Kellogg Company printed Web addresses on more than 6.5 million of its Kellogg's Corn Pops cereal packages. When customers go onto the "Gotta be Connected" webpage, they are run through a series of pop-up messages that capture personal information, along with cell phone data, including the phone number. Within days, Kellogg sends a text message with a trivia question. Those who answer the question correctly receive a free Corn Pops screensaver, as well as a chance to win additional prizes, including "pre-paid airtime, a free phone or other prizes."

Behavioral Profiling

Database marketing has become a core strategy for companies targeting teens, and a linchpin of many digital media campaigns—not only on the Internet, but also on cell phones, video games and other new platforms. Marketers can compile a detailed profile of each customer, including demographic data, purchasing behavior, responses to advertising messages, and even the extent and nature of social networks. Marketers use the information to create messages tailored to the psychographic and behavioral patterns of the individual.

The "growth and health of our database marketing efforts have been a secret weapon for us to jump-start programs and have a continuous dialogue with our best consumers," John Vail, Pepsi's director of digital media and marketing, told iMedia Connection. Using "realtime" tracking technologies, Pepsi is now "finally able to deliver high impact online advertising," Vail said.

Companies are creating elaborate viral campaigns, sometimes using "hidden messages" to lure youth into a series of games and other activities across different media, generating buzz within the online youth subculture, all under the public radar.

Coca-Cola uses a variety of techniques to track individuals' online behavior. For example, its "My Coke Rewards" program encourages consumers to use special codes from Coca-Cola products to access a website, where they can earn such rewards as downloadable ring tones and "amazing sports and entertainment experiences." This "next-generation" promotion, explained Jeff Zabin, a director at Coke's technology partner Fair Isaac, in an article written for ChiefMarketer.com, is "the most sophisticated example of how brands can utilize code promotions to capture behavioral and psychographic information about consumers." The campaign embodies the company's "vision" of "connect, collect and perfect"—"to connect with consumers, collect relevant information from consumers and, finally, perfect those relationships over time."

Digital "360" Buzz Campaigns

Peer-to-peer marketing (sometimes called "buzz," "word-of-mouth" or "viral" marketing) has become a staple among youth advertisers. Market researchers target key, influential young people who can serve as "brand sirens," promoting products to their peers through instant messaging, social networking sites and blogs. Companies are creating elaborate viral campaigns, sometimes using "hidden messages" to lure youth into a series of games and other activities across different media, generating buzz within the online youth subculture, all under the public radar. This "360" marketing strategy engages with young people repeatedly wherever they are—in cyberspace, watching TV or offline.

KFC used a high-pitched tone as a promotional "buzz" device for a recent "interactive advertising campaign." The "MosquitoTone" was embedded in TV commercials to launch KFC's new "Boneless Variety Bucket." In its press release, the company explained that the popular cell phone ring tone "is too high pitched for most adults to hear because most people begin to lose the ability to hear high frequency tones starting at age 20. This is a fact not lost on young Americans who seek the sound for clandestine ring tones that don't turn the heads of nearby adults."

In the TV commercial, the secret sounds were designed to attract the attention of young viewers and direct them to a website, where they could enter a contest to identify exactly where the tones could be heard in the ad, in order to win $10 coupons redeemable for the new chicken meal at any KFC.

Sprite created an alternate reality game "Lost Experience"—based on the highly popular ABC television series, "Lost"—giving viewers an opportunity to be more involved with their favorite show while inadvertently becoming engaged in a Sprite website. Marketers began by creating a "faux-commercial" that aired during an episode of the TV series, in order to "leak" the Web address—Sublymonal.com—to viewers. Once online, site visitors were invited to participate in a scavenger hunt with "DJ podcasts, videos and hidden memos." Codes were also hidden in print ads in Entertainment Weekly and People magazines. As a result, more than 500,000 codes were entered and Sprite's Web traffic jumped 400 percent.

Infiltrating Instant Messaging

The three major instant messaging formats—AOL's AIM, Yahoo's Messenger and MSN Messenger—all promote themselves aggressively to advertisers that want to permeate and surround teenagers' ongoing casual conversations. AOL, Yahoo and MSN Messenger offer a variety of strategies, including "roadblocks" and "takeover ads" that flood a site's homepage with interactive commercials, as well as branded "bots" and buddy icons.

The "M&M Always IMvironment" features the brand's popular "spokescandies." "There's a new way to add a little more M&M to your day," the site chirps. "Chat with friends about life, love and chocolate with this cool IMV. There's an M in everyone." IMvironments are animated backgrounds that customize the appearance of an instant message window.

"Max Out your chats!" urges the Yahoo IMvironment sponsored by Kraft's Lunchables. "New Lunchables Lunch Combinations Maxed Out Double-Stacked Tacos have arrived and you're in charge of the flavor and the fun. Buzz a friend and take your chat from Mild to Wild—no salsa necessary! Try it now."

Commercializing Online Communities

Marketers have aggressively moved into MySpace and other social networking sites, taking advantage of their large, highly detailed user profiles and expanding lists of "friends," which facilitate extensive targeting. Social networks are also blurring the line between what is marketing and what isn't.

"Welcome to the King's Court," beckons the Burger King MySpace profile. "The virtual home of the Burger King. He's giving away free episodes of the Fox shows '24,' 'Pinks' and 'First Friend.' . . . And in typical King fashion, he's giving you plenty of other stuff to check out too." MySpace users can interact with the "King" on MySpace and add him as a "friend," which gives the "King" access to their personal profile with information like age and hometown.

Designed to encourage young consumers to engage playfully with products over long periods of time, many sites offer "free" content, games, merchandise and endless replays of television commercials.

At the MySpace Jack-in-the-Box profile, visitors are greeted by "Jack Box" himself, who announces that his goal is "to rule the fast food world with an iron fist." Through the profile, youth can read Jack's daily blog entry, post a poem about the joys of cheeseburgers, or create a film and send it in for a chance to win a "Jackie."

"Brand-Saturated" Environments

Food and beverage companies have created their own online branded entertainment sites, seamlessly weaving a variety of interactive content with product pitches and cartoon "spokescharacters." Designed to encourage young consumers to engage playfully with products over long periods of time, many sites offer "free" content, games, merchandise and endless replays of television commercials.

With the growth of broadband technology, these digital playgrounds have evolved into highly sophisticated "immersive" experiences, including entire programs and "channels" built around brands. Multicultural marketers are keenly aware of the strong interest in music particularly among African American and Hispanic/Latino youth, and have created branded entertainment featuring popular celebrities and offering free downloads of their recordings.

Burger King created its own "branded online channel," called Diddy TV, using popular rapper P. Diddy's celebrity pull to draw viewers to the Burger King site.

The Mars candy company enlisted the musical group Black Eyed Peas to make a series of "webisodes" called "Instant Def," in order to promote Snickers bars to teens. The brand is featured prominently in the storylines.

Viral Video

Short online videos are an increasingly popular way of promoting brands among youth, who like to view the videos and forward the links to their friends through IM, text messaging and blogs. Marketers are creating their own "viral videos" to promote their brands through peer-to-peer networks and video sharing services like YouTube. In some cases the sponsoring company is identified, while in others it is disguised.

Wendy's placed several viral videos on YouTube, specifically designed to attract "young consumers." In one video, "Molly Grows Up"—which generated more than 300,000 views—a young girl orders her first Junior Bacon cheeseburger and Frosty. While Wendy's own corporate name was not connected to the intentionally humorous videos, users who watched them were sent to a special website for "Wendy's 99-cent value menu."

In January 2007, Domino's Pizza revealed that it was behind a viral video that had received millions of hits. To promote its "Anything Goes Deal Contest," the company placed a series of viral videos on MySpace and other popular social networking sites, using characters offering to sell big-ticket items. The first video, "MacKenzie Gets What MacKenzie Wants," featured a "spoiled rich girl who wanted a blue car for her birthday but got a red one instead. Her whining persisted until she got the car she wanted and then, much to the surprise and delight of video viewers, she decided to offer her red car on eBay for only $9.99," according to a Domino's press release, which revealed the company as the creator of the video. The campaign was a hit, according to Domino's. "With over 2 million views across multiple video sites, the popularity of the MacKenzie videos earned a top spot on several video sharing websites," the press release stated.

Recruiting "Brand Advocates"

With more young people creating their own online "user-generated content," marketers are now encouraging them to "co-create" and promote commercials for their favorite brands. In marketing circles, two new buzzwords—"consumer-generated" and "brand-generated" media—are often used interchangeably, suggesting an intentional blurring of roles.

The strategy is designed to foster powerful emotional connections between consumers and products, tap into a stable of young, creative talent willing to offer services for free and produce a new generation of "brand advocates."

At General Mills' Millsberry.com website, children are encouraged to make the "best movie" about "Lucky" (of Lucky Charms cereal) and then vote for the winning video. The site provides a pre-branded kit of settings and spokescharacters, making it easy to combine them into a personalized commercial.

Pizza Hut's contest invited pizza enthusiasts to create a short video, "demonstrating their devotion to Pizza Hut Pizza" and showing why they should earn the title of "Honorary Vice President of Pizza." Contestants were encouraged to engage in a variety of creative acts to show their loyalty to the brand, such as "decorating their room with Pizza Hut memorabilia." Entrants submitted their videos on YouTube, ensuring they would be seen by thousands of viewers, whether they won or not.

"Game-vertising"

In-game advertising, or "game-vertising," is a highly sophisticated, finely tuned strategy that combines product placement, behavioral targeting and viral marketing to forge ongoing relationships between brands and individual gamers. Marketing through interactive games works particularly well for snack, beverage and other "impulse" food products. Coca-Cola, Pepsi, Mountain Dew, Gatorade, McDonald's, Burger King and KFC, for example, were the "most recalled brands" by video game players, according to an October 2006 survey conducted by Phoenix Marketing International.

Not only can marketers incorporate their brands into the storylines of popular games, they can also use software that enables them to respond to a player's actions in real time, changing, adding or updating advertising messages to tailor their appeal to that particular individual. At a September 2006 conference on interactive advertising, software developers explained how they purposefully create games to make them "in sync with the brand," ensuring that images players see in the game are similar to what "they see in the supermarket aisle . . . [and on TV] Saturday morning." In presentations at the conference, developers said that games must always be "addictive," should include a "viral component" and be "continually updated" to facilitate ongoing data collection and analysis.

Sony partnered with Pizza Hut to build the ability to order pizza into its "Everquest II" videogame. If a player types in the command "pizza," Pizza Hut's online order page pops up, allowing the player to place an order.

At Viacom's Neopets.com—targeted at 8- to 17-year-olds—young gamers create and "take care of" virtual pets, earning virtual currency (neopoints) to pay for the pet's upkeep by participating in contests and games. The site earns substantial advertising revenues from "User Initiated Brand Integrated Advertising"—activities or games built around advertisers' products and services that help build relationships and generate revenues with Neopets visitors. For example, participants can earn points by buying or selling "valuable commodities," such as McDonald's French fries, or winning games with names like "Cinnamon Toast Crunch Umpire Strikes Out." Food companies that have sponsored various activities on Neopets include McDonald's, Frito-Lay, Nestlé, Kellogg's, Mars, Procter & Gamble, General Mills, Kraft Foods and Carl's Jr./ Hardees.

Advertising Through Avatars

Immersive three-dimensional environments are on the cutting edge of digital marketing. These "virtual worlds" are complex, multilayered enterprises that combine many of the most popular online activities—such as instant messaging, interactive gaming and social networking—into increasingly elaborate settings in which individuals create their own online identities through avatars.

"Once the stuff of science fiction," explains the website for the new-media ad agency Millions of Us, "virtual worlds are becoming central to the future of marketing, technology, entertainment and brand-building."

Marketing through avatars is "one of the most effective kinds of advertising going," wrote Jesse Shannon, president of the premiere interactive marketing agency, SAJE Media, on an interactive advertising website. He explains that the speed with which a "brand or marketing message can spread through a virtual world from avatar to avatar is breathtaking." Among the food and beverage brands actively engaged in avatar-based strategies are Coca-Cola, Pepsi, Kellogg, Nabisco, Kraft, Pizza Hut, P&G and Subway.

Habbo Hotel—"a teen community where you can meet people, play games and create your own online space"— aggressively promotes itself as a marketing venue, providing "companies and brands with a completely new and exciting way of building their brand value among teenagers around the world," according to a Habbo press release. Marketers can sponsor various elements on the site, and Habbo Hotel's pre-programmed avatars have been designed to make replies involving specific promotions.

Among the "Quests & Activities" currently featured on the home page of Habbo Hotel is a promotional game for Kellogg's Pop-Tarts. "The Crazy Good Pop-Tarts Pastries are Hollywood Bound," the site announces. "Find out where they are now!" Hotel inhabitants are also offered virtual incentives to take part in a poll: "Just for voting, you'll have a chance to receive one of 20 free RARES [Habbo furniture]!"

MyCoke.com is a virtual, immersive environment that offers a multitude of interactive activities to engage teens, including chat, music downloading and mixing, user-generated video, blogs and its own currency. Coca-Cola worked with interactive marketing expert Studiocom to create Coke Studios, a "massive multiplayer online environment" where "teens hang out as their alter-identities, or 'v-egos.'" Teens who want to become part of the MyCoke community are greeted with encouraging step-by-step instructions on the site: "Ready to reinvent yourself?" "Be who you want with your v-ego." After users complete the registration process the site exclaims: "You've just made millions of new friends! People are cool. We'll help you meet more of them."

A Pervasive Presence

Marketing has become a pervasive presence in the lives of children and adolescents, extending far beyond the confines of television and the Internet into an expanding and ubiquitous digital media culture.

Food and beverage companies are at the forefront of a new 21st century marketing system. The strategies and techniques the companies are employing in this new arena mark a dramatic departure from traditional advertising. For example, in-game advertising is not just a new form of product placement; it is a highly sophisticated interactive environment designed to closely monitor individual players, as well as direct personalized ad messages designed to trigger impulsive purchases. Viral marketing is not just an online extension of word-of-mouth brand promotion, but also a calculated database strategy that relies on detailed profiles of key "influentials," along with surveillance of their social networks. And so-called "brand-generated marketing" is not a way to direct advertising messages to children, but instead an increasingly popular method for recruiting millions of children to create and distribute the ads themselves.

> *[T]hese new food marketing strategies, designed to intrude into every possible "touchpoint" of a young person's daily life, make it very difficult for children to maintain health.*

These emerging patterns and directions raise a number of troubling issues. While choices about what to eat are always made within a larger context, these new food marketing strategies, designed to intrude into every possible "touchpoint" of a young person's daily life, make it very difficult for children to maintain health.

The digital media system is still in a formative, fluid stage, however. There is no question that digital media are also playing a positive role in the lives of young people, in many diverse ways. And while the growth and expansion of the interactive marketing system will continue unabated, there is time for the public, parents, health advocates and policymakers to be sure the new media culture serves the health of children rather than undermines it.

5

Teens May Not Respond to Online Advertising

Mark Dolliver

Mark Dolliver is a writer and former editor-at-large of AdWeek.

Despite their immersion in technology and social media, teens may not be receptive to online advertising. According to recent research, this age group is frustrated with marketing efforts that interfere with social networking and its conveniences. As for on-line gaming sites, players are judgmental of the relevance of ads and their authenticity to the experience. Marketers overeager to reach teens through the Internet risk negative reactions to brands. Furthermore, they underestimate the power of television; in this older medium, young people expect commercials and are more open to advertising messages.

Teenagers are a mystery to most adults. New technology and media are another mystery to many adults. Combine these mysteries and you have ample opportunity for adult misperception of how teenagers use and feel about new technology and media. Some recent research works to get beyond popular misconceptions and provide a look at how teens actually engage with these things, including the advertising they encounter along the way.

Based on quantitative and qualitative research conducted between January and April [2009], a report released last month [September 2009] by GTR Consulting confirms the conventional wisdom that teens are deeply involved in social networking. But it raises serious doubts about how congenial a medium this has been for marketers trying to reach the teen audience. Asked to cite the online activities they indulge in during their free time, 66 percent of the teens said they "use social networks"—exceeding the number who said they "watch user-generated videos" (59 percent), "send or receive instant messages" (51 percent), "play online games" (50 percent), "watch TV/movie clips" (36 percent), "get news/current events" (34 percent) or "blog" (12 percent). The report emphasizes that social-networking sites "have become more important for communication and connection among teens than the telephone, e-mail or instant messaging."

But that doesn't necessarily mean teens constitute an audience for marketers when they're visiting social sites. "Notably, we found that teens use social networks to socialize, not to read ads, play games or participate in marketing efforts," says the report. Indeed, GTR finds teens critical of online advertising more generally. "They know that advertising is the price to pay for getting online services for free," says the report, "but after spending hours online each day, they have grown weary of the many variations of online marketing. . . . From banner ads, online billboards, pop-ups and advergames to fictitious brand profiles on their social networking pages, teens universally point to these marketing efforts as their least favorite aspect of the Web."

A report released in the spring by youth-marketing agency Fuse (in tandem with the University of Massachusetts at Amherst) found a similar aversion to advertising via social sites. One part of its polling, fielded in June, asked teens to say how they'd like brands in various categories to advertise to them. Ads on social-networking sites ranked poorly across a range of sectors. For instance, just 10 percent of respondents said they like apparel brands to reach them via social networking, vs. 71 percent saying they like those companies to use TV spots; 14 percent said they like consumer-electronics companies to advertise to them via social networking (vs. 69 percent saying the same about TV spots); 11 percent like getting food and snacks marketing messages via social networking (vs. 78 percent citing TV).

Advertisers that treat social networks like billboards, TV, radio, or other media in which they simply run advertising will be met with at best a neutral reaction from teens and can be met with real backlash.

Risking Backlash on Social Networks

Since social networking is so important to teens, do brands risk an out-and-out backlash if they blunder intrusively onto that turf? Gary Rudman, president of GTR Consulting, suggests that they do. "If brands are clumsy and fail to understand how teens want to be approached in the social-networking environment, marketers are risking a potentially hostile reaction," he tells AdweekMedia. As for online advertising more broadly, he adds that teens are "frustrated by ads that disrupt, distract and disturb their online experience." Or, as GTR's report puts it, "From what teens have told us, online advertising is interruptive, distracting and intrusive. In a nutshell, online advertising is not working for this generation."

Bill Carter, a partner in Fuse, has also seen wariness of marketers' ventures into social media when these are out of sync with the reasons teens go to these sites. "Teens are indifferent to advertisers on social networks who don't participate in the actual purpose of the social network, which is to actively communicate with each other and have fun in their communities and organized groups," says Carter. "Advertisers that treat social networks like billboards, TV, radio or other media in which they simply run advertising will be met with at best a neutral reaction from teens and can be met with real backlash."

That's not to say it's impossible for marketers to create a rapport with teens via social media. "Advertisers that are proactive members and participate as any good 'friend' does will be engaged by teens," says Carter. Rudman notes that teens turn to social networks in part for "efficiency" in conducting their lives, and marketers that serve this end can use social media to their advantage. "One teen stated that social networks make their social life easier to handle," he notes. "If a marketer can create and offer a branded app that can make their online experience more efficient, teens are more likely to appreciate the brand and may even forward the tool to their friends," Rudman adds.

Rudman also stresses the effectiveness that can come from a marketing approach that lets teens feel they've "discovered" the brand or its message. "If teens feel like they've discovered something, they're so apt to pass it on," he says. "They feel so empowered when they feel they've discovered it on their own."

Judgmental of In-game Advertising

Along with social sites, video games and online gaming sites have become important venues for teens to use their free time. And, of course, this has lured marketers who wish to reach teens on their home ground. But this entails its own challenges. In the case of online gaming sites, the broadening of the gaming audience beyond its youth-oriented roots can be a complicating factor. Rudman mentions that teens who go to such sites are frustrated by the proliferation of ads that have nothing to do with their own interests. "If you have a Depends ad there, it's obviously not relevant to teens," he remarks.

Teens also bring a judgmental eye to in-game advertising. Says Carter: "Teens apply much the same authenticity test to in-game advertising as they do to other media. Is the advertising authentic? Is it credible? Does it belong in the game? Is it a distraction? Does it bring something positive to the game experience? If an advertiser can pass this test, it will be met with either a neutral to slightly positive response from teens. If the advertising fails this test, the best the advertiser can hope for is a neutral response, and the more likely response is disdain."

The Efficacy of Television

In their eagerness (or, at times, over-eagerness) to connect with teens via newer media, marketers may be underestimating the efficacy of an older medium: television. For one thing, despite their immersion in new media, teens still spend plenty of time watching TV—2.1 hours a day, according to the GTR report, a shade more than the 2 hours per day they spend online "for fun." (They spend another 1.4 hours a day online "for school work," or so they say.) And, what's at least as important, TV is a medium where teens aren't congenitally averse to encountering advertising. "When it comes to options for advertising, traditional TV advertising resonates best for teens," says the GTR report.

"Marketers that fail to emphasize television in their marketing efforts risk missing the boat with teens," says Rudman. "Teens are visually literate, and a good television ad will engage them. They remember funny, interesting, engaging, unique ads. In fact, if they like them enough, they will look for them online, such as on YouTube, so they can forward them on to their friends."

Perhaps surprisingly, TV's utility for reaching teens extends to products that have come along in what some people imagine to be the post-TV age.

GTR's findings are consistent with those of Fuse Marketing's survey. Seventy-five percent of the teens polled by Fuse agreed that TV is the "best way" for advertisers to reach them. The teens also ranked TV as their favorite platform for messages from all the advertiser categories about which they were asked, ranging from health and beauty to quick-serve restaurants.

Carter says that noticing which media teens consume is "the easy part" for marketers. "The difficult part is deciphering in which media teens are inclined to listen to a brand's message versus those media they consider more sacred and want free from advertising." Nobody ever accused TV of being sacred, and Carter identifies it as a medium "in which teens are open to an advertiser's message." Perhaps surprisingly, TV's utility for reaching teens extends to products that have come along in what some people imagine to be the post-TV age. Thus, when the GTR polling asked teens to say where they "typically learn about electronics and technology," 56 percent included TV among their sources, putting it slightly ahead of "online" (56 percent) and outpointed only by word of mouth (77 percent).

Technology Adoption Is in Teens' DNA

Those numbers are particularly telling when one considers the importance of technology in the lives of today's teens, for better or worse. The GTR survey found 21 percent of its teens agreeing at least somewhat that "I have experienced peer pressure to have and use the latest technology." But that phenomenon does not translate into any general aversion to new technology. One reason for this: 76 percent of the teens polled by GTR agreed (including 42 percent agreeing strongly) that "Technology helps me socialize/communicate with friends." In other words, it is integrated into daily life for teens in a way that is generally not the case for their elders, even if the latter make ample use of new technologies.

"When it comes to technology, it's almost universal that teens are not ambivalent about adopting it," says Rudman. "In fact, technology adoption is part of the teen DNA. They have grown up in a world where technology drives communication and social interaction. They must jump on board so they don't fall out of the loop. They really do not know any other approach. But although they are pushed on board, they quickly wrest control of new technology and make it their own."

The numbers in GTR's report certainly make it clear that engagement with multiple technologies is more the rule than the exception for teens. Given a list of electronic products and asked to say which ones they have, majorities pointed to the cell phone (85 percent), video-game console (79 percent), TV (79 percent), desktop computer (76 percent), digital camera (69 percent), portable gaming device (56 percent) and MP3 player with video (51 percent).

Or, teens may decide that a particular technology simply isn't for them. This is what has happened with Twitter, suggests Rudman. "Teens as a whole have rejected Twitter as a tool for adults," he says. "Twitter seems to be an announcement to the world, while things like Facebook and texting are a way of announcing to the people they care about."

One wild card in how teens will interact with the world around them is the recession. As is the case with respect to consumers in general, marketers are wondering whether the severe downturn will have a lasting effect on teens, persisting even after the economy has recovered. Carter suspects that it will. "Teens are observing an economy with real consequences," he says. "Maybe one or more of their parents have been laid off, maybe they hear the conversations about not being able to pay a mortgage on time, maybe they won't go away to summer camp or on a family vacation this year. In any case, their lives have been affected, and they are not going to soon forget the significance of what they are feeling."

6

Text Messaging Can Be an Effective Marketing Tool to Reach Teens

Alana Semuels

Alana Semuels is a journalist for the Los Angeles Times.

With teens using their cell phones for information and entertainment more and more, a growing number sign up to receive ads and pitches via text message. In fact, youths are twice as likely as adults to trust mobile marketing, resulting in a higher rate of responses, or "click-throughs" to text messages than to Internet ads for this age group. Recognizing the potential for resistance and backlash, brands and companies offer useful, engaging information to teens in text messages, from dating advice to downloadable widgets to event alerts. Nonetheless, there is sometimes very little difference between the types of promotional text messages teens will accept and those they will reject.

As she readied for last night's prom, Jamie McGraw asked her friends for advice about hairstyles, shoes and a dress.

She also turned to her cellphone for a little help.

McGraw receives daily text messages from Seventeen magazine about fashion, including tips about what to wear to the prom. She planned to take the magazine's suggestion to wear a brightly colored outfit and be prepared for "dress malfunctions." "When the texts recommend a certain look that sounds good, I will try it out, but it doesn't always mean buying something," the 17-year-old Laguna Niguel resident said.

Yakking teens and phones have been inseparable for decades. The difference today is that teens use their cellphones for a lot more than just talking. It has become a palm-size entertainment and information center increasingly consuming their time and attention. Advertisers are realizing that if they want to reach teens, they need their number—literally.

"They're not watching TV, you're not reaching them in other places," said Andrew Miller, chief executive of Quattro Wireless, a mobile advertising network. "Mobile is where they congregate."

This year, shy escorts can buy (for 99 cents) a preproduced video of a guy asking a girl to the prom ("We'd take amazing prom pictures together," he says) and then send it via mobile phone to ask a girl out, thanks to Venice-based Mogreet Inc. His nervous date can visit Cosmo Girl's mobile phone site and look at the prom section to find out how to say "No" to alcohol. And she can go to PromGirl.com to download a widget that lets her browse for prom dresses on her phone without burning up valuable Internet minutes.

It may all seem a little bothersome, but teens don't mind receiving messages about products on their phones, says Nic Covey, director of insights at research firm Nielsen Mobile. Nielsen said teens were nearly twice more likely than adults to trust and respond to advertising and pitches on mobile phones.

"For them, responding to an ad that's relevant by sending a text or following a link on their phone is a logical brand engagement," Covey said. It's so natural that the student council at Notre Dame high school in Sherman Oaks decided to invite teens to their graduation via a prerecorded video sent over a mobile phone.

Being in Teens' Pockets

Not all teens are so readily accessible, of course. Molly Nadeau, a senior at Fairfax High in Los Angeles, loves the trendy and inexpensive fashions of Forever 21 Inc., but that doesn't mean she wants to be inundated with blurbs about its latest blouses or jewelry on her mobile phone.

"Once they have my number, I just think the ads would come 24/7," she said. "I wouldn't want that." That wouldn't make her father happy, Nadeau noted, since he pays the phone bill and her plan doesn't allow for unlimited text messages.

Marketers claim they are sensitive to such resistance, saying that's why they craft the ads more in terms of useful information teens would want to get on their phones.

Hearst Magazines, for instance, has developed nine different mobile sites across different magazines, including Seventeen and Cosmo Girl. Cosmo Girl's site contains information on horoscopes, gossip, fashion, career advice and beauty tips, alongside promotions from retail giant J.C. Penney Co. and cosmetics maker Clinique Laboratories. Teens can also send a text message when they see a product they like in the magazine and sometimes receive a free sample.

"We decided we needed to follow [the reader] with our brands—wherever she is, we needed to be there with her as a source of entertainment," said Sophia Stuart, director of mobile for Hearst Magazines Digital Media.

That means a prom section that gives girls advice on date etiquette and fun things to do aside from drinking and having sex. "We wanted to help her have a script and be there if she needs our help," Stuart said.

Other brands are messaging their way into teens' phones as well. Teens interested in Element Skateboards can sign up for text message alerts when there are skate events in their area, or when stores get new products. Those who want to be in the know about clothing retailer G by Guess can get text messages about sales and promotions.

"You have to take an active role in integrating a brand into consumers' lifestyles by being in their pockets," said Roman Tsunder, president of Access 360 Media Inc., which recently launched promotions for Guess Inc. and Element that encouraged teens to sign up to get text messages on their cellphones from the companies.

[B]rands that target the teen audience [with text messaging] are looking at more authentic ways to insert themselves into the conversation, as opposed to advertising.

Teens don't seem to mind the text messages they receive from the retailers. Tsunder said only 4% of people who sign up for the texts ask to stop getting them. And Miller said 2% to 4% of those who see or receive ads on mobile phones click on them to find out more information. On the Internet via computers, so-called click-through rates are generally closer to 0.01%.

Some teens do mind, however, if advertisers bug them too overtly, said Alyson Hyder, media director for California at Avenue A/Razorfish, a digital marketing firm.

"They will be quick to turn on the backlash," Hyder said. That's why "brands that target the teen audience are looking at more authentic ways to insert themselves into the conversation, as opposed to advertising."

For a Nintendo Co. campaign, rather than send teens an ad about a new Nintendo game, mobile-phone marketing firm Hyperfactory published a brain teaser relating to it in game magazines. Users sent a text message to get the answer, and they received a message back with a link to sign up for alerts about the game and download free wallpaper and mobile games. The company declined to say how many consumers participated.

When Kiwibox.com, an online teen magazine, launches a service to send teens text messages with horoscopes and celebrity alerts this year, they'll include a short advertisement at the end sponsored by different brands such as Sparq Inc., a company that designs workout training programs for aspiring athletes, and Paramount Pictures.

The Thin Line of Product Pitches

But it can be a thin line between the type of product pitches that teens will accept on their mobile phones and those they won't.

Quentin Brown, an 18-year-old high school senior from Santa Monica, said he texted to vote during the National Basketball Assn.'s slam-dunk competition at this year's All-Star game. In return, he received a flurry of text messages with offers to buy jerseys and other basketball-related stuff. He didn't mind the texts for the jerseys, since he's interested in them and always looking for deals. But he didn't like getting ones about things he didn't care about, such as asking him to join an NBA fantasy draft or go to NBA summer camp.

"They were kind of stalking me," he said. "But then they stopped and I was glad."

7

Alcohol Advertising Does Not Significantly Influence Teen Drinking

Statistical Assessment Service (STATS)

Founded in 1994, the Statistical Assessment Service (STATS) is a nonprofit, nonpartisan organization that examines statistics in the media.

Studies used to support the direct link between alcohol advertising and teen drinking are conflicting and confusing. While research has established that ads have a small, even marginal, impact on teen drinking and attitudes toward alcohol, cause and effect cannot be proven. And in theory, alcohol advertising itself is only effective in persuading consumers to switch brands, not increasing consumption. On the other hand, peers, parents, and risk-taking behavior are major factors influencing teen drinking. The prices of alcohol and proximity of campuses to liquor-serving establishments are also strongly correlated with binge drinking among college students.

Anti-alcohol advocacy groups such as the Center on Alcohol Marketing and Youth (CAMY), the National Center on Addiction and Substance Abuse (CASA), and the Center on Alcohol Advertising (CAA) regularly assert in reports and studies that alcohol advertising leads to underage drinking. The cumulative implication of this research is that such advertising should be restricted. But the problem is that when the overall body of research on the relationship between advertising and underage drinking is analyzed the evidence of a direct link disappears.

Two reviews by the National Institute on Alcoholism and Alcohol Abuse (NIAAA, 1995 and 2000) did not find the evidence for a link compelling. As the NIAAA reported in its *10th Special Report to Congress on Alcohol and Health*, (2000) there is "very little consistent evidence that alcohol advertising influences per capita consumption, sales or problems."

The real world would appear to back the NIAAA. The 2009 National Institute of Health (NIH) report *Monitoring the Future* found that that the annual prevalence for both "any use of alcohol" and "been drunk" declined slightly for 8th, 10th, and 12th graders between 2002 and 2007—a period when alcohol advertising increased. Furthermore, The National Survey on Drug Use and Health reported that during the same period, current use of alcohol by 12- to 17-year-olds decreased significantly and did not change for 18- to 20-year-olds.

The reason for the gap between advocacy research and weight-of-evidence reviews of the full research is that the studies purporting to show a link between advertising and underage drinking rely on confusing, often contradictory data. Plus, the many factors involved in trying to measure the effect of advertising on alcohol consumption make this a complex and difficult issue to study.

Advertising theory tells us that while advertising is useful in getting consumers to switch brands or to purchase a more expensive brand it does a poor job of increasing *total demand* within an industry. In fact, the total advertising elasticity of demand for beer has been calculated at 0.0—meaning advertising has no impact on total demand. Companies advertise for a specific product, and when they do see an increase in demand, it is at the expense of a competitor. This is why companies spend billions of dollars each year on advertising: they want a larger share of the pie: they are not making a bigger pie.

Understanding the Kinds of Research

The divergent position of advocacy research means we need to understand why certain kinds of research provide more reliable evidence than others.

Experimental Research

Experimental research provides controlled testing of causal processes. In the case of underage drinking following exposure to alcohol advertising, researchers must control for variables such as education and after school supervision in order to eliminate their effects.

Researchers have found either no effect or a small, short-lasting effect on attitudes towards drinking following alcohol advertising but have not found a casual link between alcohol advertising and underage drinking. It is important to note that attitudes about drinking rather than actual drinking behavior are measured.

Survey Research

Survey research uses questionnaires and/or statistical surveys to gather data about specific behaviors and attitudes.

The survey research shows that parents and peers are the overwhelming causal factor in underage drinking, along with a young person's tolerance for risk taking. Study results show a relatively strong association between drinking or drinking initiation and a weak-to-nonexistent relationship to advertising. When non-advertising variables are analyzed, peer drinking is always one of the stronger variables and a young person's appetite for risky behavior is also strong.

Econometric Research

Economic Research uses regression analysis to look at the relative impact of potential causal variables; in this case, researchers analyze consumption in relation to advertising spending, advertising restrictions or alcohol policies.

A survey of other econometric studies [studies that use statistics and mathematical formulas to examine economic problems and theories] found alcohol advertising exposure to have an extremely small impact on alcohol consumption, particularly when compared to the effects of peer drinking. Price was shown to have a greater influence on youth consumption than advertising.

Reviewing the Research

The 2009 Roper youth Report, (5) which annually conducts 1,000 face-to-face interviews, asked students what influences them most about their decision to drink or not drink alcohol: 68 percent responded "parents" while 11 percent responded "best friend." Only 2 percent said that "what they saw in the media" (radio, TV, magazines, etc.) influenced them and another 2 percent said that "advertising" most influenced them. Just as important, for those students who were employed, the "parents" figure dropped to 45 percent while the "best friend" percentage increased to 26 percent.

Only 2 percent said that "what they saw in the media" (radio, TV, magazines, etc.) influenced them and another 2 percent said that "advertising" most influenced them.

Researchers have also examined the effect of alcohol branded merchandise and underage drinking. A 2006 article analyzing the relation between ownership of an alcohol branded item by middle school students and initiation of alcohol use found that students who own an alcohol branded item are 1.5 times more likely to initiate drinking relative to students who do not own alcohol branded merchandise but that peer drinking has the largest impact on a student's decision to drink. Among students whose friends drink alcohol,

50 percent themselves initiate alcohol use. Such a student is 18.6 times more likely to begin drinking than a student whose friends do not drink. . . .

A 2007 Journal of Adolescent Health article found that while alcohol branded merchandise is associated with both drinking and the intention to drink, the advertising variables are weak. Peer drinking, parental approval, friend approval, deviance, impulsivity, low religiosity and sports activity were all shown to be stronger indicators than any of the advertising variables. With this in mind, the authors concluded: "Although causal effects are uncertain, policy makers should consider limiting a variety of marketing practices that could contribute to drinking in early adolescence."

A 2006 article calling for a ban on alcohol advertising through sports found that alcohol advertising had increased in the United States by 50.8 percent between 2001 and 2007, and youth exposure to alcohol advertising on television had increased by 38 percent during the same time interval.

[T]he fact that the teens who like alcohol ads are more likely to want to drink may simply reflect their pre-existing attitudes, rather than show an effect of the commercials.

However, over the same time period, The National Survey on Drug Use and Health reported that between 2002 and 2007, current use of alcohol by 12- to 17-year-olds decreased significantly and did not change for 18- to 20-year-olds. In addition, there had been no appreciable change in past-month binge or heavy alcohol use among any of the underage groups. Driving under the influence for persons 12 years or older had also decreased significantly. Similarly, Monitoring the Future reported that the annual prevalence for both "any use of alcohol" and "been drunk" declined slightly for 8th, 10th, and 12th graders from 2002 to 2007 (continuing trends observed since 1993). If increased alcohol advertising were linked to more underage drinking, these trends could not have been observed.

While the survey research consistently shows that advertising has, at most, a small effect on teen drinking and a marginally greater effect on teen attitudes about drinking, it cannot show cause and effect. As a result, it is hard to know what is really happening. For instance, while advertising may make alcohol attractive to some teens, they could just as easily enjoy or be attracted to alcohol advertising because they already hold positive attitudes towards drinking.

In other words, the fact that the teens who like alcohol ads are more likely to want to drink may simply reflect their preexisting attitudes, rather than show an effect of the commercials. The fact that the effect on behavior is much smaller than that on attitudes again shows that one cannot rely on attitudes alone to measure the real world effects of ads.

The Influence of Price

The price of alcohol has been shown to have a greater influence on youth consumption than advertising. Adolescents may be especially sensitive to price because they often have little money of their own, and those who drink heavily may not yet be addicted or may not be so addicted that they become less responsive to price changes.

In 2003, researchers looked at the relationship between local alcohol marketing rates (such as the number of bars and liquor stores located near campus) and promotions (like "all you can drink" for one price) and college binge drinking rates. They found that the greater the number of these establishments, the more college students drank. Promotions like special prices at certain times and sales of high volume containers (kegs and "party balls") were also strongly linked with increased heavy drinking.

Interestingly, this study also found that binge drinking rates were elevated when college students were more likely to be "carded" or "proofed" to verify their ages to drink at bars. While the researchers thought this might be explained by greater enforcement efforts in areas with bigger problems, it could support the argument of those who believe that a higher drinking age is likely to increase bingeing. In this scenario, under-age drinkers, fearful of being caught, buy alcohol in larger quantities when they can get it and drink it faster so they can hide the evidence.

Studies using longitudinal [studies conducted over an extended period of time] surveys have not established that advertising is a causal factor for youth drinking. A 2010 review of longitudinal studies found that many "ignore statistical problems and solutions that are well-known in econometrics, including issues of specification bias, measurement error, endogeneity (a variable is said to be *endogenous* when there is a correlation between the variable and the error term) and sample selection."

This review also found that advertising studies are not particularly robust; in other words, when these studies are fully examined there are negative, null and positive results for advertising variables, sometimes in the same study. For example, among the 63 estimates of the effects of advertising and promotion on adolescent drinking reviewed, only 21 of 63 estimates (33 percent) are statistically significant. For drinking onset, only 5 of 14 estimates for mass media are statistically significant, but 4 of these are from the same study. Furthermore, the review found little replication across studies, making assessment more difficult.

A 2003 working paper for the National Bureau of Economic Research concluded that eliminating alcohol advertising completely would reduce the proportion of adolescents who drink each month from 25 percent to 21 percent. More significantly, the study claimed that a total ad ban would reduce the population of teen binge drinkers from 12 percent of adolescents to 5 percent. But the very same year, a World Health Organization sponsored study concluded that advertising bans and other marketing regulations were among the least effective policy strategies.

While a total ban on alcohol advertising might be effective in cutting teen drinking to some extent, it would be unlikely to pass constitutional muster. Furthermore, the research evidence is so mixed that it is hard to know whether a total ban would have a significant impact. Consider, for example, the persistence of illegal drug use among teens, in the complete absence of advertising. Relying on a reduction in alcohol advertising to reduce drinking will have little or no impact.

The Alcohol Policy Index (API) data has been used in a number of recent studies to examine relationships between alcohol control policies and adolescent alcohol use. API is a composite indicator used to compare and rate the alcohol policies of different countries and generate scores (based on policies from five regulatory domains). Examining the relationship between policy score and per capita alcohol consumption, analysis revealed a strong negative correlation between score and consumption. The authors believe the study revealed a clear inverse relationship between policy strength and alcohol consumption.

It is difficult to change youth drinking without affecting the consumption of legal aged adults.

A 2007 study examined this relationship and concluded that "more comprehensive and stringent alcohol control policies, particularly policies affecting alcohol availability and marketing, are associated with lower prevalence and frequency of adolescent alcohol consumption and age of first alcohol use;" but it also found that most of the relationships between API, alcohol availability and advertising control and drinking prevalence rates were attenuated and no longer statistically significant when controlling for per capita consumption in regression analyses. This suggested, the study said "that alcohol use in the general population may confound or mediate observed relationships between alcohol control policies and youth alcohol consumption." It is difficult to change youth drinking without affecting the consumption of legal aged adults.

Far More Complex

In a forthcoming paper for the *Journal of Economic Surveys*, Jon Nelson, Professor Emiritus of Economics at Penn State, warns that "a great deal of work remains to be done if this literature is to serve as a basis for sound public policy." A lack of methodological uniformity and statistical robustness has been compounded by a "dissemination bias," whereby fundamentally weak associations are repeatedly cited until they appear to gain the force of consensus. This is particularly true of research produced by CAMY, says Nelson.

Those who sell ads for alcohol and those who oppose alcohol advertising each have their own agendas and believe advertising to be powerful force, albeit for very different reasons and to different ends. Research shows the effects of advertising to be far more complex than either side admits and ignoring this critical fact doesn't help set effective alcohol policy aimed at reducing underage drinking.

Measures aimed at increasing alcohol prices could significantly affect youth drinking, but they would also be unpopular with many adults and could even have a negative impact on cardiovascular disease if they cut moderate drinking rates among adults. Moderate drinking by adults has been found to reduce heart and blood vessel diseases, which are major killers in the older age groups. A more effective and less onerous way of cutting college drinking could be to limit the number of alcohol sellers near campuses, ban price promotions like "all you can drink," and reduce volume discounts allowed on items like kegs.

Counter-advertising could also be effective, particularly ads that illustrate the potential negative consequences of drinking that are of particular concern to young people rather than ads that rely on fear-mongering or warn of long-term dangers.

Again, counter-intuitively, adults seem to be more affected by anti-alcohol and other anti-drug public service announcements than adolescents. This may result from the fact that many such ads use fear as a tactic, which is far more effective with adults than youth.

The belief that advertising induces teenagers to drink underscores attempts by lawmakers and anti-alcohol groups to impose stricter regulation and restrictions on how alcohol is marketed.

Essentially, this research shows that young people "don't think it will happen to me." Like adults, they are genuinely shocked and dismayed by horrifying images of auto accidents, overdose victims and smokers with artificial voice boxes. Like adults, they are able to recall ads that feature such images. Yet none of this seems to influence their behavior. While most adults have learned from painful experience that they are not immune to negative consequences, youth tend to feel invulnerable (and may need to maintain these feelings in order to accomplish their developmental goals of leaving their family nest).

As a result, every "Scared Straight" type program ever evaluated has been a failure. These programs are huge hits with parents—and teens tend to say that they were profoundly affected by them—but the data consistently shows either no effect or the unintended consequence of a slight increase in the behavior the intervention was attempting to prevent.

This doesn't mean that teens are impervious to anti-drinking messages: it's just that the ads that affect them aren't the dramatic ones that gain public attention and win advertising awards. In the tobacco area, for example, studies have found that ads which focus on the immediate negative effects of smoking, like bad breath or impaired athletic performance, are more effective with youth than those which warn of the likelihood of lung cancer decades hence. Similar attention to how alcohol could make one lose control in the social situations most important to teens might be a promising approach.

The belief that advertising induces teenagers to drink underscores attempts by lawmakers and anti-alcohol groups to impose stricter regulation and restrictions on how alcohol is marketed. Though all these efforts have the laudable goal of trying to reduce alcohol abuse among young people, the science upon which they are based has yet to provide clear evidence that such restrictions—or for that matter, advertising campaigns to reduce drinking—will have much, if any, effect.

8

Smoking Advertisements Influence Teen Smoking

Robert A. Wascher

Robert A. Wascher is a senior research fellow in molecular and surgical oncology at the John Wayne Cancer Institute in Santa Monica, California, and author of A Cancer Prevention Guide for the Human Race.

Facing stricter advertising regulations and a shrinking pool of smokers, tobacco companies aggressively target preteens and teens. In recent clinical research, youths between 10 and 13 years old with one or more favorite cigarette ads were at least 50 percent more likely to take up underage smoking. Furthermore, the 2007 campaign for the "feminine" Camel No. 9 brand—which included "girls' night out" parties, gift bags, and print ads in fashion magazines—had a significant impact on adolescent girls. In addition to these efforts, tobacco companies use the same marketing strategies in developing nations, where there are few legal restrictions and programs for public health.

More than 40 years after the landmark United States Surgeon General's report on smoking, cigarettes and other forms of tobacco continue to be the leading cause of preventable death around the world. In the United States alone, tobacco causes more than half a million unnecessary deaths every year from cancer and other tobacco-associated diseases. In 2010, cancer will replace all other diseases as the single greatest cause of death, worldwide. Most public health experts attribute the rising global incidence of cancer to the ongoing increase in the incidence of smoking in the developing world.

In the United States, the incidence of smoking continues to slowly decrease (although, sadly, mostly among the male half of the population) as a consequence of increased public education efforts, as well as increasingly restrictive laws against tobacco advertising and public smoking. In response to these public health policy efforts to reduce the incidence of smoking in the United States, tobacco companies have had to become more creative in their efforts to replenish the dwindling pool of smokers in America. Thus, despite their energetic denials to the contrary, tobacco companies continue to target teens and very young adults in their advertising campaigns, because the harsh and unequivocal reality of the tobacco industry is that 80 to 85 percent of all smokers become addicted to tobacco during their pre-teen or teenage years. Therefore, following the 1998 Master Settlement Agreement, in which American tobacco companies agreed to stop directly targeting pre-teens and teens with tobacco advertisements, the Big Tobacco companies have had to become more nimble and more creative in their efforts to addict a new generation of preteens, teens, and young adults to their deadly products, while simultaneously circumventing the restrictions imposed upon them by the Master Settlement Agreement.

Targeting Teen and Adult Women

R.J. Reynolds, a huge player in the international tobacco trade, recently rolled out (no pun intended) a new brand of cigarette targeted at female smokers. "Camel No. 9," like other brands previously targeted towards teen and adult women, is distinctively packaged and designed with "feminine sensibilities" in mind. In 2007, Camel No. 9 cigarettes joined the stable of prior and current cigarettes designed and marketed to appeal specifically to females, including the notorious Virginia Slims brand (produced and marketed by Phillip Morris), as well as the Capri and Misty brands. While the Camel cigarette brand had previously been targeted at male smokers, Camel No. 9 was rolled out, 3 years ago [2007] by R.J. Reynolds, with launch parties targeted specifically at women, at nightclubs and bars around the country. These launch parties have often been described as "girls' night out" parties for women smokers, and have included free massages, free hair styling, free gift bags containing cosmetics and jewelry and, of course, free samples of Camel No. 9 cigarettes. Additionally, as with the Virginia Slims brand, and other cigarettes targeted to female smokers, full-page advertisements in glamour magazines like Vogue, Cosmopolitan, and Glamour have targeted the almost exclusively female readers of these magazines with advertisements for Camel No. 9 cigarettes. These marketing campaigns are, of course, designed not only to gain new customers among women who are already addicted to tobacco, but also, and more importantly, to increase the ranks of smokers with new recruits among current nonsmokers, and in a setting (i.e., nightclubs and bars, where alcohol is also being consumed) where nonsmokers and "occasional smokers" can be targeted by R.J. Reynolds.

A newly published clinical research study, in the journal *Pediatrics*, reveals how tobacco companies continue to effectively target highly vulnerable pre-teens and teenagers in the United States.

In this nationwide prospective study, 1,036 adolescents between the ages of 10 and 13 years were prospectively followed between 2003 and 2008. Five sequential telephone interviews were conducted during the course of this study, which included discussions of the teens' impressions of their favorite cigarette advertisements. The fifth and final interview was conducted after R.J. Reynolds' roll-out of their 2007 campaign on behalf of the new Camel No. 9 brand of cigarettes.

Advertisement Preferences and Teen Smoking

A total of 72 percent of the teenagers participating in this public health study completed all 5 telephone interviews. Not surprisingly, the teens who reported having one or more favorite cigarette advertisements were 50 percent more likely to take up smoking during the 5-year duration of this clinical study when compared to the teens who did not have any favorite tobacco advertisements. Among the boys participating in this study, the percentage of teenagers who identified any favorite cigarette advertisements remained stable throughout the 5 sequential interviews, including the fifth interview in 2008 (after Camel No. 9 was introduced by R.J. Reynolds). However, while the percentage of girls reporting a favorite cigarette advertisement also remained stable throughout the first 4 telephone interviews, this percentage jumped by a significant 10 percentage points after the marketing campaign for Camel No. 9 was unleashed by R.J. Reynolds, at the time of the fifth and final interview. Moreover, this 10 percent increase in teenage girls reporting a favorite cigarette advertisement was almost completely associated, specifically, with advertisements for the Camel No. 9 brand.

In order to maintain and replenish their customer base of active smokers, tobacco companies must continuously recruit new smokers from the most vulnerable segments of our population: pre-teens, teenagers, and very young adults.

Taken together, the results of this important public health study reveal two very concerning findings: (1) Adolescents who express a preference for *any* specific cigarette advertisements are at least *50 percent more likely* to take up smoking during their teen years, and (2) teenage girls (but not teenage boys) appeared to be significantly impacted by R.J. Reynolds' 2007 advertising campaign for its new "feminine" Camel No. 9 cigarette brand.

One does not have to be a lawyer, or a public health expert, to put "2 and 2 together, and come up with 4," with respect to the findings and conclusions of this important public health study. In order to maintain and replenish their customer base of active smokers, tobacco companies must continuously recruit new smokers from the most vulnerable segments of our population: pre-teens, teenagers, and very young adults. Although Big Tobacco companies claim to be following the 1998 Master Settlement Agreement's restrictions on advertising targeted to children and teens, the economic reality is that as older smokers die off (and, very often, due to tobacco-associated diseases. . .), these merchants of death must continually replace their shrinking pool of potential and active customers with newly addicted young customers. As the troubling findings of this clinical research study demonstrate, the advertising campaign for Camel No. 9 has not only been effective in recruiting new female converts to this brand among current smokers, but also in attracting the essential new converts from among the tobacco companies' prime recruiting demographic: preteen, teenage, and young adult females. We should not delude ourselves, therefore, by the frequent protestations of tobacco companies, that they are following both the rules and the intent of legal restrictions on advertising to preteen and teenage boys and girls, as their continued existence as commercially viable companies *mandates* that they continue to addict pre-teens and teenagers (and young adults) to their deadly products.

Marketing to the Developing World

In addition to their ongoing efforts to addict American pre-teens and teenagers to tobacco, American and multinational tobacco conglomerates have also ramped up the same aggressive and deceptive advertising campaigns that worked so well for decades in the United States, and these Big Tobacco companies are now applying these same effective (and expensive) marketing campaigns throughout the developing world, where vast numbers of potential new and existing smokers can be targeted without significant legal restrictions against such advertising (and where little or no emphasis is placed upon public health and disease prevention by local government officials, in many cases).

9

Anti-Smoking Advertisements Can Reduce Teen Smoking

Michael Eriksen

Michael Eriksen is director of the Institute for Public Health at Georgia State University and former director of the Office on Smoking and Health at the Centers for Disease Control and Prevention.

Anti-smoking campaigns geared toward young people can counter the influence of tobacco advertising and marketing. Developed as a nonsmoking "brand" to reveal how cigarette companies lie to consumers, the "Truth Campaign" shows adolescents that smoking, in reality, is dangerous, expensive, and dirty. Exposure to the campaign reduced the likelihood of starting to smoke by 20 percent, with 450,000 fewer teen smokers as a consequence. The effectiveness of the Truth Campaign is due to its hard-hitting messages and level of sophistication as well as its graphic portrayals of smoking's consequences that audiences can identify with or relate to.

Everyone knows that smoking kills, but few really appreciate the magnitude of the problem. Smoking is the leading cause of death in society, causing one out of every five deaths, and killing one out of two lifetime smokers.

Even fewer people realize that beginning to smoke is almost always an adolescent decision made in response to teenagers wanting to appear cool, independent, sophisticated and glamorous—the aspirations of every teen and the very attributes promoted for decades by cigarette companies. It is no surprise that most adolescents that smoke show symptoms of nicotine addiction and want to quit smoking, but can't, even before graduating from high school.

The real tragedy is that we know how to prevent the problem of teen nicotine addiction, but fail to act. Rigorous scientific research has shown that price increases, strict advertising restrictions and clean indoor air laws are effective in reducing smoking for everyone, but are particularly effective among young people. The research evidence also shows that counter-marketing campaigns, particularly those aimed at debunking the carefully constructed myths of the tobacco industry that make smoking appear to be the cool thing to do, are effective in reducing smoking rates and the social acceptability of smoking.

When I directed the CDC's [Centers for Disease Control and Prevention] Office on Smoking and Health, we wanted to learn how to use marketing techniques to keep kids from starting to smoke and convened an expert panel of teen marketing experts from the private sector.

Creating a Nonsmoking "Brand"

Experts from companies like Adidas, Levi-Strauss, and Proctor and Gamble—companies that sell products to teens—advised us that if we wanted to be successful in competing with the tobacco industry's multibillion-dollar effort to get people to smoke, we needed to do more than educate teens on the harm of smoking, and rather create a "brand" that would compete with the cigarette brands that appealed to young people, namely Marlboro (with its cowboy), Camel (with its Joe Camel campaign), and Newport (with its "Alive with Pleasure" campaign).

The experts recommended that the nonsmoking "brand" that might appeal most to youth was one that told the truth about smoking, i.e., that smoking really provided none of the attributes seen in the cigarette advertisements, but was in fact an expensive, dirty, smelly habit, and that the cigarette companies were simply lying to them to increase their profits.

This "brand" became known as the "Truth Campaign" and was successfully used in Florida with funds from its settlement with the tobacco industry, and was rolled out nationally by the American Legacy Foundation as an outgrowth of the 1998 Master Settlement Agreement. The Truth Campaign was unprecedented in its success. Recent analysis found that exposure to the campaign reduced the risk of starting to smoke by 20 percent, resulting in 450,000 fewer adolescent smokers, and this was done in a cost-effective manner, with every $1 spent on the counter-marketing effort resulting in a savings of $6 of future medical costs averted.

The campaign was so successful, in fact, that the Lorillard Tobacco Co. sued the Legacy Foundation to cease the campaign under the guise that the advertisements vilified them.

The tobacco industry hates the truth and hates counter-marketing campaigns that tell the truth. Why? Because it works.

Smoking is perpetuated by cigarette company marketing, and smoking can be extinguished by effective counter-marketing. But the counter-marketing has to be hard-hitting, sophisticated and appealing to adolescents and young adults showing them the "truth" about smoking and also graphically depicting how devastating smoking can be to those you care about or identify with.

The tobacco industry hates the truth and hates counter-marketing campaigns that tell the truth. Why? Because it works. Given the tobacco industry has recently been found guilty in a federal district court of racketeering and perpetuating a fraud on the American people, upheld in a May [2009] federal appeals court decision, it seems to be that there is a need for more "truth" and not less.

10

Fast Food Advertising Is Linked to Rising Childhood and Teen Obesity

American Psychological Association

The American Psychological Association (APA) is a professional and scientific organization that represents psychologists in the United States.

Increased advertising for unhealthy food products is strongly associated with rising rates of obesity in youths, which have nearly tripled in the last quarter century. Advertising that targets children is inherently exploitative; those under six years old cannot distinguish between advertisements and regular programming, and those under eight years old do not comprehend the persuasive nature of advertisements. Children, nonetheless, can recall the contents of and develop product preferences following a single commercial exposure. On television, advertising for fast food, snacks, and cereal dominate the rare public service announcements and commercials for health eating. Marketing aimed at youths online confuses advertising and information and in schools it blurs the line between education and targeting a captive audience.

The childhood obesity epidemic is a serious public health problem that increases morbidity, mortality, and has substantial long term economic and social costs. The rates of obesity in America's children and youth have almost tripled in the last quarter century. Approximately 20% of our youth are now overweight with obesity rates in preschool age children increasing at alarming speed. According to the Centers for Disease Control and Prevention, the prevalence of obesity has more than doubled among children ages 2 to 5 (5.0% to 12.4%) and ages 6 to 11 (6.5% to 17.0%). In teens ages 12 to 19, prevalence rates have tripled (5.0% to 17.6%). Obesity in childhood places children and youth at risk for becoming obese as adults and associated poor health such as diabetes, cardiovascular disease, and some forms of cancer. Prevention efforts must focus on reducing excess weight gain as children grow up.

Today's children, ages 8 to 18, consume multiple types of media (often simultaneously) and spend more time (44.5 hours per week) in front of computer, television, and game screens than any other activity in their lives except sleeping. Research has found strong associations between increases in advertising for non-nutritious foods and rates of childhood obesity. Most children under age 6 cannot distinguish between programming and advertising and children under age 8 do not understand the persuasive intent of advertising. Advertising directed at children this young is by its very nature exploitative. Children have a remarkable ability to recall content from the ads to which they have been exposed. Product preference has been shown to occur with as little as a single commercial exposure and to strengthen with repeated exposures. Product preferences affect children's product purchase requests and these requests influence parents' purchasing decisions.

Impact of Advertising and Obesity on Children's Behavioral and Mental Health

- Food industry advertising that targets children and youth has been linked to the increase of childhood obesity.

- Advertising by other industries often objectifies girls and women, contributing to body dissatisfaction, eating disorders, low self-esteem, and depression.

- Many adolescents, particularly teenage girls, have body image concerns and engage in unhealthy weight control behaviors.

- Unhealthy weight control behaviors (e.g., fasting; skipping meals; eating very little food; vomiting; and using diet pills, laxatives, or diuretics) have been found to co-occur with obesity.

- Weight bias may marginalize children and youth considered obese by their peers and teachers and place them at risk for teasing and bullying.

- Body dissatisfaction and weight-related concerns extend across all ethnic groups and weight-related stigma has been found to co-occur with depression, low self esteem, and suicidal thought.

In very young children, research has found that for every one-hour increase in TV viewing per day, there are higher intakes of sugar-sweetened beverages, fast food, red and processed meat, and overall calories.

Television Advertising and Childhood Obesity

- Obesity in children increases the more hours they watch television.

- Children's exposure to TV ads for unhealthy food products (i.e., high-calorie, low-nutrient snacks, fast foods, and sweetened drinks) are a significant risk factor for obesity.

- In very young children, research has found that for every one-hour increase in TV viewing per day, there are higher intakes of sugar-sweetened beverages, fast food, red and processed meat, and overall calories (48.7 kcal/day). Excess weight can be gained by the addition of only 150 calories a day.

- Other research has found that children who watch more than three hours of television a day are 50 per cent more likely to be obese than children who watch fewer than two hours.

- Food and beverage advertising targeted at children influences their product preferences, requests, and diet.

- The food and beverage industry has resolved to self-regulate their marketing to children, but this has not resulted in significant improvement in the marketing of healthier food (i.e., fruits, vegetables, whole grains, low-fat or non-fat milk or dairy products, lean meats, poultry, fish, and beans) to children. Almost three out of every four foods advertised to children falls into the unhealthy categories that contribute to the obesity epidemic.

- Food ads on television make up 50% of all the ad time on children's shows. These ads are almost completely dominated by unhealthy food products (34% for candy and snacks, 28% for cereal, 10% for fast food, 4% for dairy products, 1% for fruit juices, and 0% for fruits or vegetables). Children are rarely exposed to public service announcements or advertising for healthier foods. . . .

- Clearly, children between ages 8–12 are receiving the highest rates of ad exposure. They are entering a critical stage of development where they are establishing food habits, making more of their own food choices, and have their own money to spend on the types of food they enjoy.

Online Marketing of Foods to Children

- Marketing of food to children on the internet is even more complex since the boundaries between content and pure advertising is often less clear than on television. Only a minority of advertisers include reminders distinguishing content from pure advertising.

- One study has shown that children find it harder to recognize advertisements on websites than they do on television; 6 year olds only recognized a quarter of the ads, 8 year olds recognized half of the ads, and 10 and 12 year olds recognized about three quarters of the ads.

- The majority of food brands advertised to children on TV is also promoted on the internet and often includes online games which are heavily branded, i.e. "advergames".

- Advergames can provide a more highly involving and entertaining brand experience than what is possible with conventional media.

- Websites also contain other brand-related content such as television commercials, media tie-ins, promotions, viral marketing and website membership opportunities.

- Viral marketing is used to encourage children to talk to one another about a brand's website by emailing friends in the form of an e-greeting or invitation and inviting them to visit the site.

- Marketers also often provide brand-related items that can be downloaded or printed and saved (e.g., brandrelated screensavers and wallpaper).

- The continual branding through these sites reinforces and amplifies the product message to children, who have a remarkable ability to recall content from ads to which they are exposed.

In-School Advertising

- There is also a creeping commercialism of America's schools.

- Children spend a considerable amount of their time in school settings, where compulsory attendance makes it difficult to avoid exposure to commercial content.

- Commercial content delivered in schools may be assumed to have the tacit endorsement of respected teachers and school officials, thereby enhancing the effectiveness of the advertising.

- Advertising and marketing in schools takes several forms:

- a. Direct advertising in school classrooms (via advertiser-sponsored video or audio programming)

- b. Indirect advertising (via corporate-sponsored educational materials)

- c. Product sales contracts (with soda and snack food companies), and

- d. School-based corporate-sponsored marketing research.

- Ads are now appearing on school buses, in gymnasiums, on book covers, and even in bathroom stalls.

- School advertising also appears under the guise of educational TV. For instance, Channel One, which is available in 12,000 schools, provides programming consisting of 10 minutes of current-events and 2 minutes of commercials. Advertisers pay $200,000 for advertising time and the opportunity to target 40% of the nation's teenagers for 30 seconds.

11

Fast Food Advertising Is Not Linked to Rising Childhood and Teen Obesity

Gary Becker

Gary Becker is a Nobel prize-winning economist and professor at the University of Chicago's Graduate School of Business. He is a contributor to the Becker-Posner Blog, *which is maintained by the University of Chicago Law School.*

Food advertising cannot be blamed for rising obesity in children and teens. Obesity has increased across all age groups and in countries with stricter controls over advertising. The two most important factors in obesity are the low price and convenience of fast food and the sedentary lifestyles of adolescents owed to more time spent on computers, browsing the Internet, and playing video games. Furthermore, studies used to examine the link between advertising and diet cannot separate the effects of exposure to commercials and watching television itself, and the demands of parents have influenced companies to market healthier foods to children.

A report this week [in December 2005] from the Institute of Medicine made the front pages of many newspapers and was reported extensively on television. Based on its examination of numerous studies of possible links between TV watching and weight gain, the report attributed a significant part of the increasing obesity among teenagers and young children to television advertising of foods and drinks with high sugar and fat content. It recommended that companies work with scientists and others to reformulate their products and ads. Some persons at the Institute of Medicine went further and raised the prospect of possible Congressional regulation of TV ads oriented toward children, even though, as we will see, the evidence provided by the report is weak and not persuasive.

Even within the domain of television, most of the research that relates television viewing to diet and to diet-related health does not distinguish exposure to food and beverage advertising from exposure to television in general.

The Obesity of Children Placed in Perspective

Before examining this evidence, obesity of children should be placed in perspective. Obesity has increased for most of the past twenty -five years among all groups and at all ages, including the elderly. Presumably, advertising of goods like Big Macs and Coke Cola has less influence over the consumption of adults, particularly that of older men and women. Moreover, obesity has grown in all developed countries, even those with much sharper controls over advertising. Obesity in the United States and elsewhere started increasing particularly rapidly in the early 1980's. Studies by economists, especially those by Richard Posner and Tomas Philipson, Jesse Shapiro, David Cutler, and Edward Glaeser, and Fernando Wilson sifted through many factors that might be responsible for this accelerated trend toward greater obesity. The two most important factors highlighted by these studies is the lower effective price of fat due to the development of efficient fast food outlets that save on time, and for teenagers a more sedentary use of leisure time due to the growth in time spent with computers, browsing the internet, and playing video games.

Exposure to Food Ads or Television

There is no doubt that McDonald's and other companies tend to increase their revenues when they raise advertising budgets—otherwise, companies would not be spending as much on advertising. But most of the increase in sales to a company when it advertises more tends to come at the expense of sales by competitors. So if Wendy's raises its advertising, sales by McDonalds and other competitors would tend to fall. To the extent that advertising mainly redistributes customers among competitors, the elimination of advertising of fast foods or sugary beverages through regulation would have relatively little effect on the overall demand for these products. As far as I could tell from examining the complex report by the Institute of Medicine, it did not include any studies (presumably because none are available) that directly looks at the effects of advertising by fast food and beverage companies on the overall consumption of these goods by teenagers and younger children. Instead, virtually all the studies available to them examine the effects on children's weight of greater or lesser exposure to television. The problem with such studies, even in the very few that are carefully designed, is that they cannot separate the effect on weight of greater exposure to advertising through watching more television from the effect on the propensity to gain weight from other activities correlated with watching TV, such as more sedentary behavior, or eating popcorn and other snacks while watching. The authors of the report recognize this serious shortcoming in a section on "Recommendations for Future Research", where they say "Even within the domain of television, most of the research that relates television viewing to diet and to diet-related health does not distinguish exposure to food and beverage advertising from exposure to television in general. This lack of relevant research severely constrains the findings that can be drawn about the influence of food and beverage marketing on the diet and diet-related health of American children and youth".

More Computers, Less Sports

A PhD study in progress by Fernando Wilson at the University of Chicago suggests that this qualification is crucial. He shows that the big increase since 1980 in children's use of time was not toward greater television viewing, for this remained rather constant during the past 25 years—and maybe has declined slightly. What increased by a lot was time spent with computers and videos games at the expense of lesser time spent at sports and other more active activities. Since advertising on computers and video games has been far less important than advertising on television, it is hard to see how the growth in obesity during the past 25 years could be explained at all by advertising toward children, unless TV advertising became much more effective than it had been. Advertisements clearly influence the demand for different goods, but they also are sensitive to the desires of consumers, including the influence of parents over what is consumed by their children. At the same time that consumers have been gaining a lot of weight, they have become more conscious about eating oats and other high fiber foods, about the vitamins added to different cereals, about the sugar content of foods and beverages, and eating other healthy foods. A study a few years ago by Pauline Ippolito and colleagues at the Federal Trade Commission found that when some parents began to want healthier cereals for their children, companies were quick to respond with new and healthier cereal brands. As soon as they were allowed to do so, they also began to advertise the healthy advantages of oat cereals and other products with high fiber content or with many vitamin supplements.

If children nowadays are heavier because they are less physically active than they used to be, or because their parents find fast food cheap and convenient, it is difficult to see how advertising by food and beverage companies are to blame. And despite the hype the study received, the Institute of Medicine's report on obesity and advertising did not present any convincing evidence that television advertising oriented toward children has been responsible for the increase in children's obesity during the past quarter century.

Organizations to Contact

The editors have compiled the following list of organizations concerned with the issues debated in this book. The descriptions are derived from materials provided by the organizations. All have publications or information available for interested readers. The list was compiled on the date of publication of the present volume; names; addresses, phone and fax numbers, and e-mail and Internet addresses may change. Be aware that many organizations take several weeks or longer to respond to inquiries, so allow as much time as possible.

Ad Council
814 2nd Ave., 9th Fl., New York, NY   10017
(212) 922-1500
website: www.adcouncil.org

The Ad Council is a nonprofit organization that works with businesses, advertisers, the media, and other nonprofit groups to produce and distribute public service campaigns. The council also conducts research in order to improve the effectiveness of its campaigns. Several research studies can be found on the website.

Adbusters Media Foundation
1234 West 7th Ave., Vancouver   BC V6H 1B7
   Canada
(604) 736-9401 • fax: (604) 737-6021
e-mail: info@adbusters.org
website: www.adbusters.org

Adbusters is a network of artists, activists, writers, and other people who want to build a new social activist movement. The organization publishes *Adbusters* magazine, which explores the ways that commercialism destroys physical and cultural environments. Spoof ads and information on political action are available on the website.

American Advertising Federation (AAF)

1101 Vermont Ave. NW, Suite 500
Washington, DC   20005-6306
(202) 999-2231 • fax: (202) 898-0159
e-mail: aaf@aaf.org
website: www.aaf.org

AAF is a professional advertising association representing corporate advertisers, agencies, media companies, suppliers, and academia. The organization protects and promotes the field of advertising. In addition, AAF's college-chapter program has 226 affiliated chapters in the United States and abroad.

Association of National Advertisers (ANA)

708 3rd Ave., 33rd Fl., New York, NY   10017
(212) 697-5950 • fax: (212) 687-7310
website: www.ana.net

ANA is a trade association that offers resources and training to the advertising industry. Its members provide services and products to more than three hundred companies that combined spend over $100 billion on advertising and marketing. The association publishes *ANA Magazine* six times each year and books are available for sale on its website.

Center on Alcohol Marketing and Youth (CAMY)

Johns Hopkins Bloomberg School of Public Health
Baltimore, MD   21205
website: www.camy.org

Based at Georgetown University, CAMY focuses attention on the marketing practices of the alcohol industry, in particular those that may cause harm to America's youth. The website features numerous reports and fact sheets on alcohol advertising and the consequences of underage drinking, including *Youth Exposure to Alcohol Advertising on Television, 2001–2009* and *Youth Exposure to Alcohol Advertising in National Magazines, 2001 to 2008.*

Children's Advertising Review Unit (CARU)

70 West 36th St., 13th Fl., New York, NY   10018

(866) 334-6272

e-mail: caru@caru.bbb.org

website: www.caru.org

As the children's branch of the US advertising industry's self-regulation program, CARU reviews ads aimed at children and promotes responsible children's advertising. It also corrects misleading or inaccurate commercials with the help of advertisers. Commentary and articles are available on the website.

Commercial Alert

PO Box 19002, Washington, DC   20036

(202) 387-8030 • fax (202) 234-5176

website: www.commercialalert.org

Commercial Alert is a nonprofit organization whose goal is to prevent commercial culture from exploiting children and destroying family and community values. It works toward that goal by conducting campaigns against commercialism in classrooms and marketing to children. News and opportunities to take action against various marketing tactics are posted on the website.

Federal Trade Commission (FTC)—Bureau of Consumer Protection

600 Pennsylvania Ave. NW, Washington, DC   20580

(877) 382-4357 (FTC-HELP)

website: www.ftc.gov

Part of the FTC, the Bureau of Consumer Protection defends consumers against fraudulent or destructive practices. The Bureau's Division of Advertising Practices protects people from deceptive advertising by monitoring advertisements for numerous products, including tobacco, alcohol, and over-the-counter drugs.

Internet Advertising Bureau (IAB)

116 East 27th St., 7th Fl., New York, New York   10016
(212) 380-4700
website: www.iab.net

The IAB is comprised of more than 375 leading media and technology companies that are responsible for selling 86 percent of online advertising in the United States. On behalf of its members, the IAB is dedicated to the growth of the interactive advertising marketplace, of interactive's share of total marketing spend, and of its members' share of total marketing spend. The IAB educates marketers, agencies, media companies and the wider business community about the value of interactive advertising. Working with its member companies, the bureau evaluates and recommends standards and practices and fields critical research on interactive advertising.

Media Awareness Network

1500 Merivale Rd., 3rd Fl., Ottawa, ON   K2E 6Z5
   Canada
(613) 224-7721 • fax: 761-9024
e-mail: info@media-awareness.ca
website: www.media-awareness.ca

The Media Awareness Network is a nonprofit organization that promotes media education and develops media literacy programs. Its Media Issues section examines topics such as marketing to children and stereotyping in advertisements. The website also provides information for parents and educators.

Bibliography

Books

Rita Clifton

Brands and Branding. New York: Bloomberg Press, 2009.

Marcel Danesi

Why It Sells: Decoding the Meanings of Brand Names, Logos, Ads, and Other Marketing and Advertising Ploys. Lanham, MD: Rowman & Littlefield, 2007.

Lilia Goldfarb

"Buying Into Sexy": Preteen Girls and Consumerism in the 21st Century. Saarbrücken, DE: VDM Verlag, 2009.

Barrie Gunter, Anders Hansen, and Maria Touri

Alcohol Advertising and Young People's Drinking: Representation, Reception, and Regulation. New York: Macmillan, 2010.

Sharon Lamb and Lyn Mikel Brown

Packaging Girlhood: Rescuing Our Daughters from Marketers' Schemes. New York: St. Martin's Press, 2006.

Sharon Lamb, Lyn Mikel Brown, and Mark Tappan

Packaging Boyhood: Saving Our Sons from Superheroes, Slackers, and Other Media Stereotypes. New York: St. Martin's Press, 2009.

Martin Lindstrom

Buyology: Truth and Lies About Why We Buy. New York: Broadway Books, 2010.

Carrie McLaren and Jason Torchinsky, eds.

Ad Nauseam: A Survivor's Guide to American Consumer Culture. New York: Faber & Faber, 2009.

Herb Sorensen   *Inside the Mind of the Shopper: The
                     Science of Retailing.* Upper Saddle
                     River, NJ: Wharton School
                     Publishing, 2009.

Karen   *Connecting Social Problems and
Sternheimer   Popular Culture: Why Media Is Not
                     the Answer.* Boulder, CO: Westview
                     Press, 2009.

Max Sutherland   *Advertising and the Mind of the
                     Consumer: What Works, What
                     Doesn't, and Why.* Sydney, AU: Allen
                     & Unwin, 2009.

Jean M. Twenge   *Generation Me: Why Today's Young
                     Americans Are More Confident,
                     Assertive, Entitled—and More
                     Miserable Than Ever Before.* New
                     York: New Press, 2007.

Paco Underhill   *Why We Buy: The Science of
                     Shopping—Updated and Revised for
                     the Internet, the Global Consumer,
                     and Beyond.* New York: Simon &
                     Schuster, 2009.

Christopher   *Always On: Advertising, Marketing,
Volmer and   and Media in an Era of Consumer
Geoffrey Precourt   Control.* New York: McGraw-Hill,
                     2008.

Periodicals and Internet Sources

Diane Clehan   "Lines Drawn for Tween Market,"
                     Variety, March 29, 2007.

Krista Conger   "Watch Not, Want Not? Kids' TV
                        Time Tied to Consumerism,"
                        Stanford Report, April 12, 2006.

Rebecca Cullers   "10 Anti-Drug Ads That Make You
                        Want to Take Drugs," *Adfreak*, April
                        29, 2011.

Rebecca Cullers   "Do Advertising Bans Deter Bad
                        Habits In Youth?" *Consumer
                        Affairs.com*, August 17, 2010.

Leah Dobkin   "Teach Your Kids to Be Consumer
                        Conscious," *Ode*, April 2008.

Stuart Elliot   "Today's Lesson: Selling Teenagers on
                        Benefits of Milk," *New York Times*,
                        September 25, 2008.

Anne Lyken   "Graphic, Repulsive Anti-Smoking
Garner   Ads: Are They Effective?" *Bizcovering*,
                        June 23, 2009.

Morgan Giangola   "Alcohol Advertisements Promote
                        Underage Drinking," *azTeen
                        Magazine*, December 2010.

Henry A. Giroux   "Commodifying Kids: The Forgotten
                        Crisis," *Truthout*, April 3, 2009.

Kenneth Hein   "Teen Talk Is, Like, Totally Branded,"
                        Brandweek, August 6, 2007.

Derrick Z.   "Targeting Youth to Start Drinking,"
Jackson   *Boston Globe*, November 20, 2010.

Sally Kalson   "Pre-teens Get Their Fill of Food Ads
                              on TV," *Pittsburgh Post-Gazette*,
                              March 29, 2007.

Cecilia Kang   "Parting with Privacy with a Quick
                              Click," *Washington Post*, May 8, 2011.

Allen D. Kanner   "Today's Class Brought to You
                              By . . ." *Tikkun*, January/February
                              2008.

Douglas   "Alcohol, Then Tobacco. Now Fast
MacMillan   Food?" *BusinessWeek*, July 1, 2009.

Haley Shuler   "The Teen Scene: The Key to Teen
                              Marketing Is All About Tapping into
                              Their World," *Impressions*, August
                              2006.

Victor C.   "Children, Adolescents, Substance
Strasburger   Abuse, and the Media," *Pediatrics*,
                              October 2010.

Harry L. Valetk   "Child-Proofing Your Ads: New
                              Maine Law Restricts Marketing to
                              Minors," Law.com, August 4, 2009.

Index

A

Access 360 Media Inc., 56
Advocacy research, 58–59
Age, drinking, 66
Age verification and binge drinking, 64
Alcohol consumption
    anti-drinking advertising, 67–68
    control policies, 65–66
    influences, 61–65
    research analysis, 58–60
American Legacy Foundation, 77
American Psychological Association, 79
Animal testing, 29
Anti-smoking advertising, 75–78
A/Razorfish, 56
Attention, 29
Avatars, 43–44

B

Becker, Gary, 86
Behavioral profiling, 35–36
Bell, Hilary, 28
Binge drinking, 63–64
Black Eyed Peas, 40
Body image, 18–19
Bonne Bell, 28–29
Brands
    alcohol brand merchandise, 61–62
    anti-smoking advertising, 76–78
    brand awareness, 7–8

brand collaboration, 23, 25
branded entertainment, 39–40
Brown, Jill, 26–27, 31
Brown, Quentin, 57
Burger King, 39, 40

C

Camel No. 9 cigarettes, 70–73
Carding for alcohol purchases, 64
Carter, Bill, 48–49, 51
Celebrity endorsements, 13–14
Cell phones, 34–35, 38, 53–57
Chester, Jeff, 33
Clothing and fashion
    brands, 7–9
    instant messaging, 53–54
    tweens, 26–32
Coca-Cola, 36, 44
Code promotions, 36
Computer use, 89
Consumerism, 10–14
Counter-advertising, 67–68

D

Database marketing, 35–36
Developing countries, 73–74
Digital media. *See* Internet; Mobile marketing
Dolliver, Mark, 46
Domino's Pizza, 40

E

Econometric research, 60–61
Economic issues, 24–25, 52
Environmental issues, 28–29

At Issue

Are Americans Overmedicated?

Other Books in the At Issue Series:

At Issue

Are Americans Overmedicated?

Tamara Thompson, Book Editor

GREENHAVEN PRESS
A part of Gale, Cengage Learning

GALE
CENGAGE Learning™

Detroit • New York • San Francisco • New Haven, Conn • Waterville, Maine • London

Christine Nasso, *Publisher*
Elizabeth Des Chenes, *Managing Editor*

© 2011 Greenhaven Press, a part of Gale, Cengage Learning.

LIBRARY OF CONGRESS CATALOGING-IN-PUBLICATION DATA

Are Americans overmedicated? / Tamara Thompson, book editor.
    p. cm. -- (At issue)
  Includes bibliographical references and index.
  ISBN 978-0-7377-5141-3 (hardcover) -- ISBN 978-0-7377-5142-0 (pbk.)
  1. Americans--Drug use. 2. Drug utilization--United States. I. Thompson, Tamara.
  RM138.A74 2011
  615'.10973--dc22
                                                          2010038102

Printed in the United States of America
1 2 3 4 5 6 7 15 14 13 12 11

Contents

Introduction

When most people think about drug use in America, they think about illegal drugs such as marijuana or cocaine. But pharmaceuticals are far more widely used than illicit drugs are, and the use of such medications has skyrocketed over the past two decades. According to a 2006 study by Boston University, 82 percent of American adults and more than half of children now take at least one medication (prescription or nonprescription drugs, vitamins or herbal supplements) every day. Nearly 30 percent of adults take five or more daily; 27 percent of children take two or more. Americans fill more than 3.5 billion prescriptions from their doctors each year, accounting for nearly half of the global pharmaceutical market.

Americans are, without question, the most heavily medicated people on the planet. But regardless of whether that illustrates a penchant for quick fixes and overly permissive prescribing—as some critics say—or whether it reflects better health screening and more accessible treatments—as the drug industry says—the forces that shape the statistics are themselves highly controversial.

The main force is the pharmaceutical industry. With $291 billion in annual sales, the pharmaceutical industry is the fastest-growing and most profitable sector of the US economy, and spending on prescription drugs is the fastest-growing category of health-care expense.

According to the nonpartisan Center for Public Integrity, the pharmaceutical industry spent $855 million—more than any other industry—on lobbying from 1998 to 2006. In 2009 the industry had 1,228 lobbyists, more than 2 for every member of Congress. Whether related to drug safety oversight, Medicare prescription coverage, or the drug-patent extension in President Barack Obama's health-care reform package (approved by the Senate in March 2010), all such lobbying is intended to translate into public policies that favor profits for pharmaceutical companies, often known collectively as Big Pharma.

Besides lawmakers, a critical focus for Big Pharma's influence is the Food and Drug Administration (FDA), the government agency responsible for regulating the testing, manufacturing, labeling, advertising, marketing, efficacy, and safety of prescription drugs in the United States. A large part of the FDA's funding comes from fees paid by pharmaceutical companies as their drugs move through the regulatory process. Many critics argue that this practice is akin to letting the fox guard the henhouse because the agency is charged with scrutinizing the products of the very people that are paying its bills. Because of its close ties to drug companies the FDA has been highly criticized in recent years for acting more like a partner of the industry than its watchdog.

Besides seeking to influence policy makers and government agencies, Big Pharma spends $3 billion a year marketing drugs directly to consumers, and another $15 billion a year marketing to doctors, who they hope will prescribe their products. While drug makers say they are simply striving to educate both the public and physicians about the benefits of their medications, critics say the real purpose and obvious result is to drive sales of drugs that may not be necessary or appropriate for an individual. Physicians are indeed increasingly likely to write prescriptions—if not because they have been influenced by drug companies, then because health insurers, including the government's Medicare program for seniors, typically cover the cost of medications, but not that of nondrug therapies that can be equally effective but often more expensive.

A good example is the antidepressant Prozac, which was quickly seen as a cost-effective replacement for psychotherapy when it was introduced to treat depression in 1988. Within five years, 4.5 million Americans had taken Prozac, and annual US sales topped out at $2.7 billion before the drug's patent expired in 2001. Prozac was the first mass-marketed "blockbuster" drug, and it reinvented the way medicines are prescribed, sold and promoted in the United States. It also reinvented the way Americans perceive mental health issues by mainstreaming treatment and ushering in a new era of popularized medications for depression and other mental disorders.

Aside from Big Pharma's massive marketing machine and an American culture primed to embrace its message, the number of people taking psychiatric drugs grew further because the *Diagnostic and Statistical Manual of Mental Disorders* (DSM-IV), the official criteria manual used to diagnose psychiatric disorders—broadened its criteria for many conditions. More easily met criteria meant more people could be diagnosed with a disorder and receive medication. As an example, when the criteria for attention-deficit/hyperactivity disorder (ADHD) was broadened, critics allege, many healthy but very active children easily met the threshold for diagnosis. Sales of ADHD drugs jumped nearly 500 percent in just a decade. By 2004 some 2.5 million American children were taking ADHD drugs, including almost 10 percent of ten-year-old boys nationwide.

According to Big Pharma's critics, another reason medication use has increased is that pharmaceutical companies have literally invented new diseases for their pills to treat. An example of such a practice is the drug Detrol for "overactive bladder," a condition that did not exist until the drug maker coined the term and then spent millions teaching doctors how to recognize it. Detrol has since turned into a blockbuster drug, with annual sales of $1.2 billion. "We are taking too many drugs for dubious or exaggerated ailments," says physician Marcia Angell, former editor of the *New England Journal of Medicine.* "What the drug companies are doing now is promoting drugs for long-term use to essentially healthy people. Why? Because it is the biggest market."

Drug makers, however, explain their stellar sales growth by saying it is a matter of better treatment options. "We now have more medicines and better medicines for more diseases," says Jeff Trewhitt, a spokesman for the Pharmaceutical Research and Manufacturers of America (PhRMA), a trade organization that represents the country's leading pharmaceutical and biotechnology companies.

Whether such heavy and widespread medication use is appropriate or whether Americans are overmedicated is an ongoing controversy, but a growing number of doctors, researchers, and public health experts believe that, whatever the case, the pharmaceutical industry must be reformed. In her book *Our Daily Meds*, Melody Petersen, a former pharmaceutical industry reporter for the *New York Times*, sets forth a plan to do just that. Among her ideas:

- A law should be enacted that prohibits doctors from accepting money or gifts from pharmaceutical companies, which likewise should be prohibited from giving them.

- The government should establish an independent agency to keep the research interests of science and the public good separate from the profit-driven motives of pharmaceutical companies.

- To undo a deeply entrenched conflict of interest, the FDA should no longer be supported by fees paid by pharmaceutical companies.

- Because under-the-radar promotion is far more powerful than direct advertising, practices such as using celebrity spokespeople, having sales reps promote medicines directly to doctors, and letting drug companies sponsor public events, disease screenings, and physician education should be banned.

Whether implementing any or all of these suggestions would alter the number of pills Americans take is unclear, but many believe that reforming the industry's practices would be an important first step toward reducing the undue influence of drug companies and bolstering consumer protection. The authors in *At Issue: Are Americans Overmedicated?* represent a wide range of viewpoints concerning the consumption of pharmaceutical drugs and the forces that shape their widespread use and cultural acceptance.

1

Americans Take Too Many Prescription Drugs

J. Douglas Bremner

J. Douglas Bremner is a physician and researcher who publishes the popular drug and health safety blog Before You Take That Pill.

Americans take more prescription medications than any other people in the world, and it is mostly because of the power and influence of pharmaceutical companies. Government deregulation and the weakening of the Food and Drug Administration (FDA) in the 1980s allowed new drugs to be approved with greater speed and less scrutiny than before; then, in 1992, fees collected from drug companies became the major source of funding for the FDA. This conflict of interest continues today, and Big Pharma's deep influence means that the FDA's decisions usually favor the profit-driven interests of the pharmaceutical industry rather than protecting consumers. The drug industry is a major marketing machine that spends more money to convince people they need drugs—and to convince doctors to prescribe them—than it does to create the drugs themselves.

The latest drive to get new pills on the shelves and into people's mouths began when government deregulation and an earnest attempt to help AIDS-HIV patients access important life-extending drugs collided. In the 1980s there was a

J. Douglas Bremner, *Before You Take That Pill: Why the Drug Industry May Be Bad for Your Health: Risks and Side Effects You Won't Find on the Labels of Commonly Prescribed Drugs, Vitamins, and Supplements*. New York: Avery, 2008. Copyright © 2008. All rights reserved. Reproduced by permission.

strong movement to decrease the role of government regulation in all businesses, and budgets of regulatory agencies like the FDA [Food and Drug Administration] were slashed as part of that effort. The [Ronald] Reagan Administration painted the FDA as a bloated bureaucracy that was slowing down the approval of drugs and getting in the way of business.

There was some truth to that claim. At that time it could take up to two years to gain drug approval, two years too long if you were suffering from HIV-AIDS. Throughout the 1980s, AIDS activists and patients echoed the drug companies' sentiments, complaining that it took too long to bring disease-fighting drugs to market. The pharmaceutical industry lent a sympathetic ear and a loud voice to calls for speed in approvals of AIDS drugs such as Agenerase (amprenavir). Since drugs are on patent for a limited number of years, every year spent waiting for approval from the FDA meant losing a year of profits.

Couple that with the fact that the FDA could now honestly say that, because of cuts, it was understaffed. The answer was essentially legislation allowing pharmaceutical companies to pay the salaries of the staff at the FDA. In 1992, the Prescription Drug User Fee Act (PDUFA) stipulated that a fee (now $576,000) be paid to the FDA by the pharmaceutical companies for each new drug application. The number of staff at the Center for Drug Evaluation and Research (CDER) doubled overnight. Today, the FDA receives about $260 million a year from these fees. Part of the bill stipulated that funding by Congress for new drug evaluations had to increase by 3% per year. Since the overall funding for the FDA did not increase at 3% per year, the FDA had to actually cut funding for surveillance and research of approved drugs.

Conflicts of Interest

Another interesting phenomenon resulted from the change in law: the boundaries between the drug companies, FDA, and doctors became increasingly blurred. FDA officials sometimes move to jobs in the pharmaceutical industry, which means they may not want to burn their bridges with industry. The same FDA officials who approve the drugs are responsible for monitoring them after they are on the market, which gives them an obvious disincentive to say that the drugs they earlier certified as safe were now unsafe. Finally, the FDA gets input from outside advisory panels made up of doctors who are experts in their fields. Most of these doctors receive payments as consultants, research grants and support for travel to conferences from drug companies. In some cases, the doctors are working as paid consultants to the same companies whose drugs are coming up for approval by their advisory committees.

For instance, as reported by *USA Today* on October 16, 2004 ("Cholesterol Guidelines Become a Morality Play") eight of the nine doctors who formed a committee in 2001 to advise the government on cholesterol guidelines for the public were making money from the very same companies that made the cholesterol-lowering drugs that they were urging millions of Americans to take. For example, one of the committee members, Dr. H. Bryan Brewer, was the Chief of the Molecular Disease Branch at the National Institutes of Health [NIH]. He worked as a consultant or speaker for 10 different pharmaceutical companies, making over $100,000 over three years while he was on the committee, and sat on one of their boards (*Los Angeles Times*, December 22, 2004, "The National Institutes of Health: Public Servant or Private Marketer?"). Dr. Brewer left the NIH in 2005 in the midst of adverse publicity about potential conflicts of interest. Nassir Ghaemi, MD, a psychiatrist at Emory University, was quoted in the *Emory Academic Exchange* (February, 2007) as saying, "Critics say we are being influenced and don't realize it—that drug companies are smarter than we are and know a lot more about human psychology than we think, and they're probably right about that to some extent."

Increasing Pressure to Prescribe

Expert consensus guidelines have a potent effect on doctors; they can be held liable if they do not adhere to accepted standards of care. Dr. Curt D. Furberg, a former head of clinical trials at the National Heart, Lung, and Blood Institute and now a professor at Wake Forest University in North Carolina, explained how such information reached physicians: "The [company] reps tell the doctors, 'You should follow these guidelines,' implying that you're not a good doctor if you don't follow these guidelines." (*Los Angeles Times*, December 22, 2004, "The National Institutes of Health: Public Servant or Private Marketer?)"

To gain the most market share, companies have to invent drugs for diseases that previously had no treatment . . . or create prevention medications for alleged risks.

The result of this co-mingling was a boon for drug makers, approval time of their products decreased from 20 months to six months right after the law changed. However, the number of drugs that had to be later withdrawn also increased from 2% of drugs to 5% of drugs.

There is another troubling dichotomy that could have terrible repercussions for our health: while the number of people with disease is not growing, the number of adult Americans taking medication is increasing—half of us take prescription drugs and 81% of us take at least one kind of pill everyday—and that percentage is expected to rise in the coming years. To gain the most market share, companies have to invent drugs for diseases that previously had no treatment (or treat problems that may not necessarily require drug treatment, such as "restless leg syndrome"), or create prevention medications for alleged risks (like the risk of fracture in the elderly) by expanding the potential pool of medication takers. That meant moving from the realm of giving medications to sick people, to giving medications to people who looked well, but might be at an increased risk based on the result of a blood test or some other hidden marker of disease. Thus the era of disease prevention and risk factor modification was born.

The US is the only country in the world where you can turn on the TV and have an announcer tell you to go 'ask your doctor' for a drug.

To promote this shift, for the past two decades the pharmaceutical industry has pushed educational programs, which they claim are designed to identify people in need of treatment or prevention with medication. This is usually done by donating money to organizations who advocate on behalf of a specific disease who will in turn "get the word out," increasing public awareness and screening, and expanding the number of individuals who will potentially take the medication. This is fine for identifying individuals with undiagnosed high blood pressure or to detect the early stages of colon cancer. But awareness campaigns are not always meant to be purely, altruistically educational. Most are linked to a drug company's marketing campaign.

Benefits Questioned

There are a number of conditions for which we are now urged to obtain screening and potential treatment, including high cholesterol, osteoporosis, hypertension, diabetes, and undetected heart disease. However, the potential benefit of medications to treat these conditions is often exaggerated, side effects are minimized, and in some cases recommendations are applied to people based on evidence from different groups of people (e.g. women with risk factors for heart disease are urged to take cholesterol-lowering medications based on studies in men). In addition, doctors who work as paid consultants to the pharmaceutical industry often write the guidelines about who should take the drugs, so it is unclear how unbiased their recommendations really are.

Another factor that has expanded use of prescription medications happened in 1997, when the FDA lifted the ban on direct to consumer advertising along with the law that required ads to list every possible side effect. Soon after, Americans were bombarded daily with commercials for prescription drugs. The US is the only country in the world where you can turn on the TV and have an announcer tell you to go 'ask your doctor' for a drug. Doctors often will give medications to patients even if they don't think they need it. For example, one study showed that 54% of the time doctors will prescribe a specific brand and type of medication if patients ask for it.

A Bleak Diagnosis

With so many of us popping pills or gulping down spoonfuls of medicine, it's not surprising that more of us report related adverse effects. One hundred thousand Americans die every year from the effects of prescription medications. Over a million Americans a year are admitted to the hospital because they have had a bad reaction to a medication. About a quarter of the prescriptions that doctors write for the elderly have a potentially life threatening error. Many of these people are getting medications that they don't need, or for problems that can be appropriately and safely addressed without drugs. For example, most cases of adult onset diabetes can be prevented and possibly cured with a change in diet alone—and with considerably fewer negative side effects and numerous healthy ones, like weight loss, and lower blood pressure and cholesterol. . . .

Drugs Do Not Improve Outcomes

I'm not saying that some drugs don't ever successfully prevent disease, or that newly described diseases and syndromes are necessarily invalid. But the fact is that no matter how you look at it, the US (and to a lesser extent other countries) has a prescription drug problem. The US spends two times more on drugs, and takes twice as many drugs, as other countries, and has worse health. That means we are paying money for drugs that are not working for us.

It is time for Americans to rethink the role of medications and other pills in their lives in relation to other actions that can be taken to maximize health.

Despite the fact that Americans spend twice as much on health care as any other country in the world, we have some of the worst healthcare outcomes in the industrialized world, including total life expectancy, and survival of children to their 5th birthday. In a survey of 13 industrialized nations, the US was found to be last in many health-related measures, and overall was 2nd to the last. Countries with the best health care included Japan, Sweden, and Canada, in that order. Factors that were thought to explain worse healthcare outcomes in the US included the lack of a developed and effective primary care system and higher rates of poverty. Even England, which has higher rates of smoking and drinking and a fattier diet, has better health than the US. . . .

It is time for Americans to rethink the role of medications and other pills in their lives in relation to other actions that can be taken to maximize health, such as making changes in diet; incorporating exercise into one's daily routine; learning and using stress reduction techniques; and changing other behaviors like quitting smoking. The most common disorders, like diabetes and heart disease, are always better treated and prevented through changes in diet, exercise, and lifestyle than they are with medication. Pharmaceuticals can be life saving for some conditions, such as insulin for Type I diabetes, thyroid hormone for hypothyroidism, or antibiotics for life threatening infections. All of this has been shown through several scientific studies. Before you take that pill, consider taking charge of your health by making informed decisions and smart changes in your lifestyle. In some cases, however, you may need medications for prevention or treatment of disease, or to help you with troubling symptoms or disabilities. In those cases you should know as much as you can about the risks and benefits, so that when it is time to talk to your doctor you can make an informed decision that both of you are happy with.

2

Prescription Drugs Help Millions Live Better Lives

Pharmaceutical Researchers and Manufacturers of America (PhRMA)

The Pharmaceutical Researchers and Manufacturers of America (PhRMA) is a lobbying organization that represents the country's leading pharmaceutical research and biotechnology companies.

Advances in medical science have led to important medications that help people live longer and healthier lives. Drugs for HIV have drastically reduced the death rate from AIDS; cholesterol-lowering statin drugs have reduced the need for invasive heart surgeries; blood-thinning drugs help prevent devastating strokes; diabetes medicines help people avoid serious complications from that disease; and anticancer drugs have increased cancer survivor rates and added 10.7 percent to life expectancy at birth for Americans. Because medicines can prevent or manage diseases, overall health-care costs are lower as people do not need as many expensive treatments, hospitalization, or surgeries. Medicines also benefit the economy because people lose fewer days of work and are more productive when they take medications for their health problems. The pharmaceutical industry also contributes to economic stability by creating thousands of jobs ranging from sales representatives to scientific researchers.

Over the last few decades, scientists have made substantial progress in the discovery of new medicines. Even more dramatic advances are anticipated in the years ahead through research in new fields such as genomics and proteomics.

In the last decade alone, over 300 new medicines have been approved by the FDA [Food and Drug Administration]. These advances are improving the treatment of common diseases like heart disease, diabetes, and cancer, as well as rare disorders like Fabry's disease, cystic fibrosis, and sickle cell anemia.

As a result of these new discoveries, medicines are taking on an increasingly important role in patient care. As a result, we are spending more on pharmaceuticals. In return, more patients are living longer, better lives; overall health care costs are restrained as patients avoid invasive surgeries and costly hospital and nursing home stays; and the economy is strengthened through improved worker productivity.

Studies Confirm Value of Medicines

A growing number of studies are confirming the increasing value of new medicines to patients and society. For example, a study by Frank R. Lichtenberg, the Courtney C. Brown Professor of Business at Columbia University, finds that patients using newer drugs were significantly less likely to die and lose workdays than those using older drugs. Lichtenberg also found that the use of newer medicines increased drug costs by $18, but reduced hospital and other non-drug costs by $129,[1] meaning that for each additional $1 spent on newer pharmaceuticals, $6.17 is saved in total health care spending, $4.44 of which comes from savings in hospital spending.

New Medicines Save and Improve Lives

- New medicines have made a major contribution to the decline in the death rate from HIV/AIDS in the U.S. over the last 10 years. Since the mid-1990s, when re-

21

searchers developed a new wave of medicines to treat HIV/AIDS, the U.S. death rate from AIDS dropped about 70%.[2]

- Several studies have found that use of statin therapy to treat people with high cholesterol reduces hospital admissions and invasive cardiac surgeries. For example, a study of one statin showed that it reduced hospital admissions by a third during five years of treatment. It also reduced the number of days that patients had to spend in the hospital when they were admitted, and reduced the need for bypass surgery and angioplasty.[3]

- A study sponsored by the Agency for Health Care Policy and Research concluded that increased use of a blood-thinning drug would prevent 40,000 strokes a year, saving $600 million annually.[4]

- A February 2004 study by Lichtenberg finds that new cancer drugs have accounted for 50% to 60% of the gains we have made in cancer survival rates since 1975. Since 1971, when the U.S. declared war on cancer, our arsenal of cancer medicines has tripled. During that time, the survival rate rose from 50% to 67%. Overall, new cancer drugs have contributed a remarkable 10.7% of the increase in life expectancy at birth in the U.S.[5]

New Medicines Help Control Health Care Costs

- A January 2004 study by Duke [University] researchers found that "beta-blocker therapy improves the clinical outcomes of heart failure patients and is cost saving to society and Medicare." The study, which was written before enactment of the Medicare drug benefit, notes: "If medication costs were completely reimbursed by Medicare, program savings from beta-blocker therapy would remain positive."[6] Looking at the overall societal perspective, the researchers found that five years of treatment for heart failure without beta-blockers cost a total of $52,999. With beta-blockers added to treatment, total treatment costs fell by $3,959, patient survival increased by an average of about three-and-a-half months, and patients needed fewer overnight hospital stays.

- New studies are showing how newer, better medicines reduce the cost of treating people with depression. The cost of treating a depressed person fell throughout the 1990s, "largely because of a switch from hospitalization to medication," the *Wall Street Journal* said in a December 31, 2003 story on the study. The study, published in the *Journal of Clinical Psychiatry* in December 2003, found that per-patient spending on depression fell by 19% over the course of the decade.[7]

- New diabetes medicines are helping patients avoid serious complications and death, and can reduce overall health care spending. One recent study found that effective treatment of diabetes with medicines and other therapy yields annual health care savings of $685–$950 per patient within one to two years.[8] Another study corroborated these results, finding that use of a disease management program to control diabetes with medicines and patient education generated savings of $747 per patient per year.[9]

- A study of the effects of a new Alzheimer's medicine, donepezil, on costs in a Medicare managed care plan showed that, although the prescription costs for the group receiving the drug were over $1,000 higher per patient, the overall medical costs fell to $8,056 compared with $11,947 for the group not receiving drug treatment. This one-third savings was the result of reduced costs in other areas, such as hospital and skilled nursing facility costs.[10]

New Medicines Strengthen the Economy

- America's pharmaceutical companies create thousands of high-quality, U.S.-based jobs. In addition to employing over 70,000 scientists, the pharmaceutical research industry directly employs more than 315,000 Americans.[11]

- New medicines also benefit the economy by increasing worker productivity and reducing absenteeism. One study, which evaluated the effect of migraine treatment on productivity, found that more than 50% of workers who received a triptan drug injection for a migraine attack returned to work within two hours, compared with 9% of workers who received a placebo.[12]

- A study in the *Journal of Occupational and Environmental Medicine* found that patients taking a non-sedating antihistamine for allergies experienced a 5.2% increase in daily work output in the three days after receiving the medication, compared with a 7.8% reduction in work output for workers receiving sedating antihistamines.[13]

- The National Committee for Quality Assurance (NCQA) says that "if every American with depression received care from a health plan or provider that was performing at the 90th percentile level, employers would recover up to 8.8 million absentee days a year."[14] NCQA also reported that only 40.1% of patients with depression "received effective continuation phase treatment."

Notes

1. Frank R. Lichtenberg, "*Benefits and Costs of Newer Drugs: An Update*," (Cambridge, MA: National Bureau of Economic Research, June 2002).

2. CASCADE Collaboration, *"Determinants of Survival Following HIV-1 seroconversion after introduction of HAART,"* The Lancet, 362 (2003): 1267–1274.

3. *"Cholesterol Pill Linked to Lower Hospital Costs,"* The New York Times, 27 March, 1995.

4. D.B Matchar, G.P. Samsa, *Secondary and Tertiary Prevention of Stroke, Patient Outcomes Research Team (PORT) Final Report—Phase 1,* AHRQ Pub. No. 00–N001, Rockville, MD: Agency for Healthcare Research and Quality, June 2000.

5. Frank R. Lichtenberg, *"The Expanding Pharmaceutical Arsenal in the War on Cancer,"* National Bureau of Economic Research Working Paper No. 10328 (Cambridge, MA: NBER, February 2004).

6. PA Cowper, et al., *"Economic Effects of Beta-Blocker Therapy in Patients with Heart Failure,"* The American Journal of Medicine, 116 (2004): 2 104–111.

7. PE Greenberg, et al., *"The Economic Burden of Depression in the United States: How Did It Change Between 1990 and 2000?"* Journal of Clinical Psychiatry, 64 (2003): 1465–1475.

8. E.H. Wagner, et al., *"Effect of Improved Glycemic Control on Health Care Costs and Utilization,"* Journal of the American Medical Association, 285 (2001): 2, 182–189.

9. J. Berger, et al., *"Economic Impact of a Diabetes Disease Management Program in a Self-Insured Heath Plan: Early Results,"* Disease Management, 4 (2001): 2, 65–73.

10. JW Hill, et al., *"The Effect of Donepezil Therapy on Health Costs in a Managed Care Plan,"* Managed Care Interface, (March 2002): 63–70.

11. National Science Foundation, Division of Science Resources Statistics, Survey of Industrial Research and Development: 200 (Arlington, VA: NSF, 2000).

12. R.C. Cady, et al., *"Sumatriptan Injection Reduces Productivity Loss During a Migraine Attack: Results of a Double-Blind, Placebo-Controlled Trial,"* Archives of Internal Medicine, 158 (11 May 1998.)

13. I.M. Cockburn, et al., *"Loss of Work Productivity Due to Illness and Medical Treatment,"* Journal of Occupational and Environmental Medicine, 41 (1999): 11, 948–953.

14. National Committee for Quality Assurance, State of Health Care Quality: 2002 (Washington, DC: NCQA, 2003).

3

Psychiatric Drugs Are Overprescribed

Charles Barber

Charles Barber is a lecturer in psychiatry at the Yale University School of Medicine and a senior executive at The Connection, a nonprofit social services agency in Connecticut.

The widespread use of antidepressants has changed the American psyche in deeper ways than those caused by the action of drugs in people's brains. As mainstream use of psychiatric drugs has grown more commonplace over the past two decades, mental illness and psychiatry have become everyday topics of conversation—and of popular entertainment. Because of such widespread acceptance, instead of treating the severe mental health issues for which they were invented, antidepressants are now overwhelmingly prescribed for the simple stresses and anxieties of everyday life. Americans spent more than $13.5 billion on antidepressants in 2006, and the psychiatric drug industry has become one of the most powerful industries in the world. Most of the people taking these drugs do not really need them, however. Americans are the most psychiatrically medicated people in the world, and unnecessarily so.

The size and reach of the psychiatric drug industry is staggering. It is far, far greater than most psychiatric practitioners realize and certainly greater than the drug companies would want you to know. There are various ways to measure the dimensions of the enterprise:

- 33 million Americans were prescribed at least one psychiatric drug in 2004, up from 21 million in 1997.

- The spending on antidepressants rose from $5.1 billion in 1997 to $13.5 billion in 2006; and on antipsychotics from $1.3 billion in 1997 to 11.5 billion in 2006.

- The third-best-selling antidepressant, Lexapro, has been on the market only since 2002. But 15 million Americans have already taken it.

- Nine percent of American teens have been prescribed drugs for depression.

- The products are not limited to adults, and not even to humans. In 2002, 11 million antidepressant prescriptions were written for American children and adolescents. Before 1990, outside of the occasional use of Ritalin, the medicating of kids was just about taboo. Clomicalm (known as Anafranil when taken by humans) is approved by the FDA [Food and Drug Administration] for separation anxiety for dogs. To increase their appeal for these segments of the market, Prozac and Paxil come in mint- and orange-flavored liquids, respectively, and Clomicalm is meat-flavored. A Los Angeles veterinarian estimates that 5 percent of the cats and dogs in his practice are taking psychotropic agents for their behavior.

- Zoloft's American sales—$3.1 billion in 2005—exceeded those of Tide detergent that same year.

- The worldwide sales of one drug for schizophrenia, Zyprexa—$4.7 billion in 2006—were greater than the revenue generated by the [clothing maker] Levi Strauss Co.

A Shift in Attitudes

Accompanying the sales of the drugs (indeed what has made the sales and ingestion of the drugs possible, at least in part) has been an equally dramatic attitude shift toward mental dysfunction on the part of Americans. As the drugs have sailed to the top of the charts, mental illness and psychiatry have gone from being taboo subjects to becoming almost chic.

Madness has ... become alluring and inviting and, at the very least, enormously popular.

[TV mobster] Tony Soprano takes Prozac, lithium, and Xanax (and his mother, Livia, took Prozac, and AJ, his son, is put on Lexapro, a newer antidepressant, in the show's last season.) [TV psychologist] Dr. Phil is a star. [Rapper] Eminem is on antidepressants. [Actresses] Lorraine Bracco (who happens to play Tony Soprano's psychiatrist) and Halle Berry suffer from depression; [Actress and model] Brooke Shields, from postpartum depression; and [soccer star] David Beckham, from obsessive-compulsive disorder. Hardly a week goes by without a celebrity revealing—usually in some well-chosen commercial format—their long-secret psychiatric disorder. . . .

Behavior as Biology

To further the ascent of Prozac et al. it has helped immensely that there has been a simultaneous barrage of media messages and images in the last decade informing the public that behavior is biologically dictated. There is a daily drumbeat emanating from the TV and the newspapers informing us that behavior is genetic, hardwired, strictly biological. Newspapers, which hardly reported health news thirty years ago, report study after study showing that behavior is biologically inherited and determined. Headlines scream "Man's Genes Made Him Kill, His Lawyers Claim," or ask "Are Your Genes to Blame?" . . .

Popular Psychiatry

This incessant *physicalizing* of behavior—which allows for a broken mind to be seen in roughly the same terms as a broken leg—has softened the image of psychological disturbance in general, and mental illness in particular. In this context, madness has, at times, become alluring and inviting and, at the very least, enormously popular. [American author] Sylvia Plath was remarkably prescient when she noted in her journal, while contemplating writing *The Bell Jar*, that "there's an increasing market for mental-hospital stuff."

To be sure, the most common portrayal of mental illness, both in the movies and in the headlines, is still the violent schizophrenic. But given its sordid history, the image of mental illness has quite improbably and suddenly become nearly chic. We have seen an emergence of "psychiatric chic," akin to the "heroin chic" of models and downtown artists. . . .

Shifting Statistics

In 1996, 38 percent of Americans viewed depression as a health problem, as opposed to a sign of personal weakness. By 2006, 72 percent saw depression as a health problem. In general, Americans feel much closer to mental dysfunction. In 1957, one in five Americans reported having personal fears of an impending nervous breakdown; by 1996, it was one in four.

Americans adore their prescription drugs like no other people on earth, but they really, really adore their psychiatric drugs.

In this environment, then, it is not at all surprising that Americans think that they are much crazier than people in other countries. In 2004, the World Health Organization completed a study on the global prevalence of mental illness. Based on structured, in-home interviews, an extraordinary *26 percent* of Americans reported that they suffered from any type of psychiatric disorder in the prior year—far exceeding the rates of all of the other fifteen countries. By contrast, 5 percent of Nigerians, 8 percent of Italians, 9 percent of Germans, and 12 percent of Mexicans reported having a psychiatric disorder. (The only country that came close to the United States was perennially troubled Ukraine.) Americans described themselves as being particularly vulnerable to anxiety disorders and impulse-control disorders, reporting them at double the rates of every other country but Colombia and France. Almost 8 percent of Americans reported having suffered from a serious mental disorder, a rate about three times higher than any other developed country in the survey. In reporting the story, the *New York Times* stated, bluntly, about Americans: "Most Will Be Mentally Ill at Some Point, Study Says." "We lead the world in a lot of good things, but we're also leaders in this one particular domain that we'd rather not be," said the study's lead author.

Deeply Immersed in Craziness

Americans have responded to what's in the air, and on the air, around them. They are deeply immersed in craziness. They take drugs for their perceived insanity at rates far exceeding any other country; they make movies and watch TV shows about mental illness like never before; they talk about mental illness in a newfound language; and they think they are the craziest people on earth.

> *Americans have the most luridly expensive urine in the world.*

And indeed all this drug taking is a profoundly, even outrageously, American phenomenon. Americans adore their prescription drugs like no other people on earth, but they really, really adore their psychiatric drugs. Americans are responsible for almost half of the world's prescription drug sales, but the disparity is even greater when it comes to CNS (central nervous system) agents. In 2006, Americans—about 6 percent of the world's population—bought about two-thirds of the world's psychiatric and neurological drugs. In 2006, 66 percent of the global antidepressant market was accounted for by the United States. And in 2003 approximately 83 percent of the global market for attention deficit hyperactivity disorder medications was accounted for by the United States, and mainly by U.S. children. . . .

This is not to say that mental illness isn't, in essence, a product of problematic neurotransmitters and faulty brain functioning—the evidence is overwhelming that it is—and that these drugs aren't extraordinarily effective at times for the people they were developed for, people with severe psychiatric conditions. It is and they are. I have witnessed the lifesaving impact of the drugs for people who really need them, people with true medical illnesses like schizophrenia, bipolar disorder, and major depression. Many of the severely ill clients that I worked with would not have survived without the drugs. But in our characteristic American impatience and zeal, the drugs have been hyped beyond the limits of their ability to help most people; their efficacy with very specific populations has been overgeneralized and misapplied to treat the troubles of the masses generally and upper-middle-class angst specifically; their largely unknown mechanisms of action have been made, literally, into cartoons; and their subtleties have been ignored and side effects overlooked.

Americans have swallowed it all—literally. To say that we are the most medicated nation on earth is an absurd understatement. To say that we are the most psychiatrically medicated nation on earth is a prodigiously absurd understatement. Americans have the most luridly expensive urine in the world.

4

ADHD Drugs Are Overprescribed for Children

Linda Marsa

Linda Marsa is a Los Angeles–based investigative journalist, author, and teacher specializing in science, medicine, and health.

Some 4 million American children are currently diagnosed as having attention-deficit/hyperactivity disorder (ADHD), and they consume 31 million drug prescriptions annually to combat symptoms such as disruptive or impulsive behavior, restlessness, and lack of focus. When kids act out in school, teachers, counselors, and family physicians are often quick to recommend medication to make them easier to manage. The United States uses 80 percent of the world's Ritalin, a stimulant drug for ADHD, a statistic many attribute to an overly permissive society that medicates children rather than disciplining them. While some children are truly helped by ADHD drugs, many children may not need such medication at all. The symptoms of ADHD can also come from other disorders, such as learning and information-processing deficiencies, or even stressful family situations like abuse or divorce. Giving children powerful ADHD medications rather than fully exploring behavioral problems and trying other interventions first is bad medicine, and parents should be wary of starting their kids on such drugs.

It's a rare parent today who's not familiar with the term attention deficit/hyperactivity disorder, or ADHD. Indeed, this once-obscure abbreviation is now a household word, thanks in part to the fact that the number of kids diagnosed with the condition has skyrocketed—from an estimated 150,000 in 1970, to a half million in 1985, to a whopping four million currently [as of 2005]. (It is outranked only by asthma and allergies among childhood disorders.)

Predictably, prescriptions for ADHD treatments have ballooned proportionately, rising more than 47 percent over the past five years to a current total of 31 million. The ADHD therapeutic arsenal—a $2.2-billion-a-year business—now includes a dozen drugs, the use of which has steadily drifted downward to ever-younger children.

A landmark 2000 *Journal of the American Medical Association* study revealed that use among 2- to 4-year-olds of stimulants such as Ritalin (which, paradoxically, have a calming effect on hyperactive kids) nearly tripled from 1991 to 1995; Ritalin prescriptions for preschoolers rose 49 percent from 2000 to 2003. This is especially sobering in view of the fact that Ritalin is not even approved for use in children under 6; all these prescriptions are written off-label [i.e., for other than originally approved uses].

We medicate our kids more, and for more trivial reasons, than any other culture. We'd rather give them a pill than discipline them.

Is Medication Really Necessary?

Despite the galloping increase in the use of such drugs, there is still considerable confusion as to exactly what ADHD is and how it should be treated. Part of the problem is that there is no definitive test to certify that a child has it. And because symptoms run the gamut from constant frenzied activity and disruptive, impulsive behavior to fidgeting, making careless mistakes in schoolwork, and failing to finish tasks, it's not always easy to distinguish between normal kid behavior and

ADHD. Diagnosis is still a judgment call, says Timothy E. Wilens, MD, author of *Straight Talk About Psychiatric Medications for Kids.*

In addition, the spectrum of ADHD has broadened. There are now thought to be three distinct types. The most extreme—and the one most associated with the label—is the hyperactive, impulsive child who is disruptive, can't sit still, and may be a bully or a troublemaker. Children with the second type are those who are inattentive, unable to focus, and easily distracted. The third type, and the most common one, usually combines inattention and hyperactivity.

For children whose extreme impulsivity and aggressiveness cause them to fall hopelessly behind in school and to become social outcasts, a parent's decision to medicate can be painful but clear-cut. But what about the parents of the millions of other kids who also bear the ADHD label but whose behavior is more ambiguous? These parents face thorny questions: Is their child's energy, dreaminess, or inattentiveness merely normal youthful behavior, or does it cross the line into a neurological illness? And would putting the child on drugs be a help or the chemical equivalent of handcuffs?

Behavioral pediatrician Lawrence H. Diller, MD, author of *Running on Ritalin,* believes the latter. "America uses 80 percent of the world's Ritalin," he says. "We medicate our kids more, and for more trivial reasons, than any other culture. We'd rather give them a pill than discipline them." His view is shared by many others, who chalk up the seemingly limitless numbers of antsy, disruptive kids to the failures of a permissive society that can't control its children and babysits them with MTV.

Others pointedly disagree. "ADHD has not increased, we're just identifying it better," says Steven Pliszka, MD, chief of child psychiatry at the University of Texas Health Science Center, in San Antonio. "In the past, these kids were the ones who were always being sent to the principal's office." Moreover, research shows that there is a strong genetic component to the disorder. If a child has it, the odds are good that a parent may, too (though he or she may be unaware of it).

It is easier and cheaper for a doctor to simply prescribe a pill than to direct the child to costly therapists.

But even if the data strongly suggest a biological origin to ADHD, says William E. Pelham Jr., PhD, director of the Center for Children and Families at the State University of New York at Buffalo, there is little doubt that environmental factors can nudge a latent, largely benign tendency into a full-blown disorder requiring medication. Several trends in American life have converged to whip up this perfect storm.

Schools Are Ground Zero for ADHD

Let's start with our schools. Faced with steadily dwindling resources and the need to find time for everything in state-mandated curricula, many have curtailed gym classes, even recess, where energetic kids can let off steam. Teachers, already pushed to the limit, are often unable to handle a "troublemaker" who creates chaos in their crowded classrooms—in turn putting parents under pressure to make their child conform. (Three-quarters of initial referrals for an ADHD examination originate with teachers, not parents.)

"Teachers are good at spotting a child who's different," says Mina K. Dulcan, MD, head of child and adolescent psychiatry at Northwestern University's Feinberg School of Medicine, in Chicago. And in doing so, they perform a valuable service. But it's valid to wonder whether, in the words of Barbara M. Korsch, MD, a professor of pediatrics at the University of Southern California, in Los Angeles, "we're giving youngsters Ritalin as a solution for poor classroom behavior."

Our healthcare system also helps make medication a likelier solution. Because HMOs [health maintenance organizations] and managed-care plans often either explicitly or implicitly encourage primary-care physicians to limit referrals to specialists, it is easier and cheaper for a doctor simply to prescribe a pill than to direct the child to costly therapists.

Others point the finger at the beleaguered institution of the modern family itself, with its (commonly) two working parents who may lack the stamina to create a highly structured home environment and who may not restrict television, video games, or Internet access. Indeed, a 2004 University of Washington study indicated a link between early exposure to television and attention problems in children.

Add to this mix the fact that, in the early 1990s, kids with ADHD who meet certain criteria became eligible for special services from their schools, which has meant that more kids were identified. And the debut of a new drug is usually accompanied by intensive sales campaigns aimed at doctors and TV viewers. "New drugs always mean more people get medication," explains Dr. Pelham.

ADHD Is Hard to Diagnose

Even when a child's symptoms clearly point to something beyond the normal vicissitudes of childhood, ADHD can be tricky to pin down. Depression, anxiety, bipolar disorder, dyslexia, learning disabilities, even impaired hearing or vision, can be mistaken for ADHD because the symptoms (insomnia, impulsiveness, inattention) are similar.

Other factors that can spark ADHD-like behaviors include emotional disruptions (divorce, the death of a close relative, a parent's job loss), neglect or abuse, an unstructured home environment, and medical problems such as epilepsy or hyperthyroidism. Sleep apnea also triggers ADHD-like symptoms, according to recent research by Ronald Chervin, MD, a sleep researcher at the University of Michigan, in Ann Arbor. "If kids don't get undisturbed sleep," he says, "they're naturally going to be inattentive and less able to learn."

The obvious first step in helping a child is to obtain an accurate diagnosis. Given the murkiness of ADHD, such accuracy requires several hours of careful evaluation, not a 15-minute office visit and a rush to medicate because a teacher complains that a child is disruptive. As tempting as it may be to give a child a pill to see whether he improves, this is poor medical practice. As Dr. Wilens notes, a positive response to a Ritalin-like stimulant does not mean a child has ADHD—these drugs can have the effect of making anyone who takes them more focused (ask any college student who has used Ritalin to cram for finals). . . .

American Academy of Pediatrics Guidelines

To help experts distinguish ADHD from other conditions, the American Academy of Pediatrics have devised guidelines, including the following:

- Symptoms must meet the criteria for the disorder established by the American Psychiatric Association. . . .

- Behaviors must create a genuine impairment in at least two areas of the child's life. If the only problem is in the classroom, it is more likely to be a learning disability than ADHD.

- Symptoms must have persisted for at least six months and have seriously interfered with the child's friendships, school activities, home life, and overall functioning.

Such evaluations typically cost anywhere from $600 to $2,000 and may be covered by health insurance. Federal law also requires [a] public school to provide both free evaluations and remedial classes for eligible kids with ADHD. . . .

A Story of Misdiagnosis

Patricia Mark's son Nicholas was diagnosed with ADHD at age 8, after his third-grade teacher noticed he didn't pay attention, had trouble reading, and wrote illegibly. "He'd have these momentary staring spells," recalls Mark, 45, a mother of three in New Milford, Connecticut. "And though he could spell any word in his head, the letters would be all jumbled when he put them on paper."

The school district referred her to a psychologist, who attributed Nicholas's symptoms to ADHD and suggested he take Ritalin. Convinced in her gut that this diagnosis was wrong, Mark refused to give her son drugs. She spent six years consulting one specialist after another. Finally, a neurologist ordered a brain scan, which revealed that Nicholas suffered from mild epilepsy. Earlier tests indicated he also had dyslexia.

Tutoring and special-education classes have helped Nicholas cope with his learning disability, but Mark feels that the boy, now a senior in high school, will never recover academically from the years he lost. Still, she remains grateful that she trusted her instincts. "Ritalin can trigger seizures," she says. "If I had done what the 'experts' advised, it might have killed him."

Drugs Can Turn a Child's Life Around

From the moment her daughter, Juliet, was born, Leslie Pia knew she was different from other babies. She cried inconsolably, rarely slept, refused to stay in her stroller, and buzzed with nervous energy. By age 2, Juliet's fierce temper tantrums made her a social pariah among her peers. "None of the mothers wanted her around their children," recalls Pia, an event planner in Plainview, New York. As the terrible twos progressed into the even-worse threes, Pia realized that Juliet wasn't going to outgrow her erratic behavior, so she and her husband, Steven, had her evaluated by a private psychologist. The verdict: Juliet suffered from ADHD.

The psychologists broached the possibility of medication, but the Pias were adamantly opposed. "I was appalled at the idea of a child barely out of diapers popping these powerful pills," says Pia, who notes that even experts are unsure what long-term effects these medications may have, especially when they're given at such a key stage of neurological development (the brain undergoes the majority of its growth during the first five years of life).

Instead, Pia scaled back her work schedule to spend more time with her daughter, read everything she could find about ADHD, and learned behavior-modification techniques. She even tried occupational therapy to tame her unruly child, who wandered around during circle time at her nursery school, bullied her classmates on the playground, and had trouble transitioning calmly from one activity to another.

"These methods would work temporarily, but nothing had a lasting effect—her brain and body were just moving too fast," Pia says. "Since I couldn't sit in the classroom with her all day long, nursery school was just a horror."

As Juliet prepared to enter kindergarten, the desperate couple made the "harrowing decision" to give their daughter the stimulant Concerta. As heart-wrenching as it was to "give my 5-year-old a pill in her applesauce," recalls Pia, the effects were immediate and dramatic. Suddenly, Juliet could sit calmly and do her work without making a fuss; she could play peacefully for short periods with other kids.

The girl, now 7, still attends behavioral therapy to improve her social skills, but "there is just no comparison to the way she was before," marvels her mom.

Parents Face Pressure to Medicate Kids

Sheila Matthews's nightmare began when her son entered first grade. His teacher phoned regularly to complain about the boy's disruptive behavior—he would blurt out answers and refuse to sit still. His teacher assigned him a special seat away from his classmates and used negative and positive reinforcements to try to curb his disruptions.

"All she was doing was stigmatizing and humiliating him," recalls Matthews, a mother of two in New Canaan, Connecticut. "This was a kid who had loved school and was always excited about learning. Suddenly he was telling me he hated school and hated himself. He was only 6!"

In all but the most severe cases, ADHD can be treated as effectively with intensive behavioral coaching as with medicine.

The school psychologist diagnosed the boy with ADHD and urged his parents to consider medication. "The psychologist told me, 'if you don't medicate him, research shows he'll self-medicate with drugs and alcohol,'" says Matthews. "I was frightened and horrified." Convinced the school district was trying to sedate her son to make him easier to manage, Matthews stood firm.

She believed her child was merely outgoing and energetic, and that drugs would dampen his natural high spirits. Instead, she paid $2,000 for an evaluation by a private psychologist, who determined the boy had trouble with sequencing, reasoning, and comprehension. This diagnosis qualified him for special speech and language services through the school district. She also enrolled him in an after-school program in third and fourth grades that helped build communication skills.

Her persistence paid off. Her son, now 12, is bringing home B's on his seventh-grade report card and learning to play guitar. "When he started doing better academically, his behavioral problems diminished," Matthews says.

In all but the most severe cases, ADHD can be treated as effectively with intensive behavioral coaching as with medicine, according to advocates such as Dr. Pelham. Most no-drug programs emphasize the use of goal setting, organizational skills, and time management. Children with ADHD need consistent rules, a high degree of daily structure, and stern consequences for misbehavior. . . .

Side Effects of ADHD Drugs

ADHD medications work by changing the levels of brain chemicals such as dopamine and norepinephrine, which help modulate activity in the parts of the brain that regulate attention, impulse control, motor activity, and organization. But what do these drugs do to [a] child's body?

While medication is sometimes the only answer for kids with severe ADHD, it's important to realize that these drugs can carry serious side effects, including insomnia, appetite loss, upset stomachs, and tics—and even, according to the most recent research, possible depression in adults who took Ritalin as kids. A small percentage of kids are also vulnerable to a "rebound effect" when the drugs wear off in the late afternoon and symptoms resurface.

While medication is sometimes the only answer for kids with severe ADHD, it's important to realize that these drugs can carry serious side effects.

Experts point out, however, that this problem has largely been eliminated in recent years. In rare instances, youngsters may experience seizures, or their growth may be affected when they continuously take medication. Most experts advise against the continuous use of these medications, especially for years on end. And many advocate that [a] child take a medically supervised "vacation" from medication at least once a year to see how he or she fares without it.

5

ADHD Drugs Are Appropriately Prescribed for Children

Hannah Seligson

Hannah Seligson is an author and journalist based in New York City.

Investigative journalist Judith Warner set out to write a book about the overdiagnosis and overmedication of American children for attention-deficit disorder (ADD) or attention-deficit/hyperactivity disorder (ADHD) and other mental health issues, but when she started doing research for the book, she concluded that kids are not overmedicated at all. According to the National Institute of Mental Health, only about 5 percent of American children take some type of psychiatric medication, and just 3 to 5 percent have an ADHD diagnosis. The media are responsible for raising a false alarm and perpetuating the myth that children are being improperly medicated. One reason the number of children on medications is growing is because of better diagnostic testing and treatment options. While many other therapies are available for ADHD and other disorders, they cannot entirely replace medication for most children. Parents who choose medication for their children understand that the benefits outweigh the risks.

Aren't all kids on some kind of medication? Isn't everyone diagnosed with something these days? Isn't ADD as common as the sniffles?

Not really, says Judith Warner, author of the new book *We've Got Issues: Children and Parents in the Age of Medication.* Warner is best known for outing the culture of overparenting in her first book, *Perfect Madness: Motherhood in the Age of Anxiety,* and her Domestic Disturbances column on *The New York Times* Web site, and now she's decided to quiet the cacophony of misconceptions about children, medication, overdiagnosing, and overmedicating in one confident hush.

How does Warner do it? She starts by challenging her own beliefs.

When she began writing her book, almost five years ago [in 2005], she came to it thinking the narratives the media had spun about children and medication were true: Parents were trying to "perfect" their children through various cocktails of medications; doctors were going prescription-happy; and kids who occasionally got sad were being labeled "depressed."

Assumptions Not Borne Out

"Those assumptions, however, weren't borne out by clinicians, parents, children, or statistics," says Warner, who did lots of research to support her thesis.

Here's what the numbers teach us:

About 5 percent of kids take psychiatric medication and, depending on how one reads the data, anywhere between 5 and 20 percent of kids today have mental-health issues. We are not a Ritalin nation. According to The National Institute of Mental Health, attention deficit disorder occurs in about 3 to 5 percent of school-age children.

The overmedicated and overdiagnosed child, Warner argues, is a media embellishment. And it's become an obsession and storyline that eclipses the realities.

We've Got Issues spotlights a bigger problem: the lack of medical care for many children with mental issues. With an overwhelmed mental-health industry—there are only 7,000 child psychiatrists in the U.S., mostly concentrated in urban areas—those who need help often don't get it. Mental-health issues have been portrayed as a bourgeois malady because that is the only segment of our population that can afford to have them. The full battery of tests to get a diagnosis costs about $2,000, which insurance companies often do not reimburse. Warner takes a stab at offering some policy solutions, including a clarion call for insurance companies to reimburse families for diagnostic tests and to increase the number of child psychiatrists.

She quotes John March, a Duke University psychiatrist, as saying, "Child psychiatry will really be the heart of psychiatry in the future. Epidemiology now shows that if you're mentally ill as an adult, you first were mentally ill as a child or an adolescent."

We've Got Issues is a reality check that separates the perceived outrages from the genuine ones, and for this alone Warner provides a real service.

The increased diagnosis and treatment for ADHD may be a major public health success story.

Areas of Controversy Still Remain

Warner is saying "bring it on" to all the dicey, controversial, and murky areas that obscure the subject of children and medication, and she's not afraid to acknowledge the issues on which there isn't consensus, including whether there really are more children with mental issues today than there were 30 years ago. "I don't know if there really are more, or we are just recognizing them more," says Warner.

Still, she devotes a chapter to exploring the topic. One of the more intriguing explanations is "assortative mating," a theory that researchers say could be one explanation for the mysterious surge of autism in our time. The theory is that today kids are getting a "higher genetic load" because people are now marrying mates who are similar to them. "Even one generation back you didn't have a physicist marrying a physicist," says Warner. Dr. Demitri Papolos, an associate professor of psychiatry at the Albert Einstein College of Medicine, says that in the past "spousal selection took into consideration knowledge of the partner's family . . . now few couples have much of a clue as to the medical and psychiatric history of families they are marrying into."

A Thoughtful Look at Medication

As for medication, Warner doesn't get righteous; she looks at the facts.

In 2005, Darshak Sanghavi, chief of pediatric cardiology and an assistant professor of pediatrics at the University of Massachusetts Medical School, wrote a piece for *The Boston Globe* under the headline "Time to calm down about Ritalin," arguing "the increased diagnosis and treatment of ADHD may be a major public health success story."

A lot of medications do work, not all parents are making their children into sacrificial lambs to their own ambitions, and a number of children do suffer from mental health issues.

Taking Warner's trademark nuanced tone, *We've Got Issues* comes down on Sanghavi's side. "I talked to one doctor who is trying to retrain the cerebellum, I talked to one doctor who believes in transcendental meditation, and I have read about many other alternative treatments, and all of them said these therapies can supplement medication, but most of the time for most children they don't end up replacing medication entirely," says Warner.

Statistics and studies aside, Warner humanizes the issues for the reader. Throughout the book she introduces parents of children whose lives were saved by medication: children who used to scream and kick for four hours while they did their homework were able, with the help of the right medication, to do it in half the time without the temper tantrums; children who might never have been able to emancipate (read: go to college) if they hadn't been on mood stabilizers.

Validating Parents' Experiences

Warner, however, is anything but glib—that's virtually impossible in a book that has close to 50 pages of notes—about medication, and *We've Got Issues* certainly isn't a paean to the prescription pad, but, like a good journalist, she sees it from all sides.

"I can understand why parents think medication is scary," she says. "It hasn't been around long enough and it can have terrible side effects, but many parents get to a point where they feel it is unfair to the child not to be on the medication, where they come to feel the benefits outweigh the risks."

The book is most successful at changing the narrative about children with mental-health issues. Of course there are pill-pushing parents, overdiagnosing psychologists, fraudulent drug companies, and irresponsible doctors, but there's another truth that Warner shakes out: A lot of medications do work, not all parents are making their children into sacrificial lambs to their own ambitions, and a number of children do suffer from mental health issues. Parents will find solace in seeing their own experiences validated on Warner's pages.

6

Ads Do Not Significantly Increase Demand for Unneeded Medications

Brian Alexander

Brian Alexander is a California-based writer who covers health issues for msnbc.com. He is the author of Rapture: How Biotech Became the New Religion.

Pharmaceutical companies spend more than $5 billion annually to advertise prescription drugs in the United States. The practice has been heavily criticized by those who believe the ads entice people to ask their doctors for unnecessary or ineffective drugs—and that doctors, in turn, are likely to prescribe them. But a recent study shows that the public is less influenced by drug advertising than it used to be. The study found that—despite the ever-increasing number of drug ads—half as many patients requested prescriptions for specific drugs when they visited their doctors in 2009 than they did in 2003.

The pharmaceutical industry says this shows that the primary effect of prescription drug advertising is not selling more drugs, but patient education that positively increases people's awareness of diseases, symptoms, and possible treatments.

Watching TV news could make you think America faces a crisis of irritable bowels, malfunctioning genitals and insomnia. The pharmaceutical industry spends billions of dollars each year to make sure you know about these, and other, conditions.

But a new study appears to show that all those direct-to-consumer ads for prescription drugs to treat such conditions have much less effect than previously thought, a finding that could be bad news for pharmaceutical companies and the media outlets with which they advertise.

Only 3.5 percent of patient visits to a group of Colorado doctors' offices and public health clinics included a patient request for a prescription for a specific drug, says the study, published in the *Annals of Family Medicine*. This was about half the rate reported in a somewhat comparable study from 2003.

The marketing of prescription medications has been controversial since 1997, when the government loosened restrictions on drug ads. Prescription drug advertising, allowed only in the United States and New Zealand, has exploded in the years since. It now tops $5 billion annually, according to a report by TNS Media Intelligence, a marketing research firm, though spending began falling off in 2007.

Advertising Sparks Debate

Debate about the practice has exploded, too. Drug companies argue that advertising medications provides an important public health service by alerting consumers to potentially undiagnosed, or undertreated, disorders. Some doctors and health advocates, on the other hand, argue that ads entice patients to insist on unnecessary or ineffective drugs and to forgo healthy lifestyle changes that might obviate the need for drugs in the first place.

The new study supports both sides.

Twenty-two primary care practices in Colorado participated. The researchers surveyed 1,647 "patient encounters"—appointments. During those appointments, 58 patients, or 3.5 percent, asked about obtaining a prescription for a specific drug. When the data was sifted to include only queries about specific drugs that had been advertised in recent years, the number fell to 43, or 2.6 percent.

Not Doctor's First Choice

Importantly, when a patient did ask about a specific drug, that drug was usually not the doctor's first choice of treatment. "Nevertheless," the study found, "the physician prescribed the [requested] medication about one-half the time."

This does not necessarily mean doctors are caving in and practicing bad medicine, said Dr. Richard Kravitz, a professor and vice-chair of research in the Department of Internal Medicine at the University of California–Davis, and an investigator on the 2003 study.

"It might be bad if it is more costly, but it is not as bad clinically as it sounds," Kravitz explained. "A lot of decisions in medicine have no clear right or wrong."

Indeed, doctors in the new study described the "overall effect of the patient request as neutral or positive in 90 percent of the visits."

The study's lead author, Dr. Bennett Parnes, an associate professor of family medicine at the University of Colorado School of Medicine, described the results as surprising. "It is not the dreaded event where you have to deal with a patient who wants medications the provider does not want to prescribe. It is just not happening that much."

Patient Education Is the Result

Half the time there was a specific patient drug request, Parnes said, a new condition was identified and there was "some patient education going on. That's not a bad thing."

But Dr. Lisa Schwartz, an associate professor of medicine at Dartmouth Medical School who has long studied consumer drug advertising, isn't persuaded. She pointed out that the Parnes study population, which included a number of community health centers serving a low-income population, may not be the best measure. Such health centers often have limited drug choices, and the patients may not have had as much exposure to drug ads.

"(That) makes it hard to make strong inferences that direct-to-consumer advertising does not work," Schwartz said.

Worrying about frequency of requests may miss the point, she said. It may be more important to know if consumers who do request a drug truly understand what they're asking for. Many ads, she argued, do not include enough information on how well drugs work.

"If it is supposed to be educational for consumers, why doesn't the ad contain that piece of information?" she said.

In the wake of recalls for drugs like Vioxx, Americans may be more skeptical of what they see advertised.

The sleep drug Lunesta, for example, advertised with a gentle moth floating in through a bedroom window, gets patients to sleep 15 minutes faster after six months of treatment and provides 37 minutes more sleep per night. Patients ought to have that information, she said, to help judge whether the cost is justified.

Consumers Are More Discerning

Parnes speculated that if the rate of requests for drugs is falling, it could be because Americans and their doctors have become inured to drug advertising. "Clinicians 10 years ago may have been shocked by a patient asking, but now they are comfortable with hearing it and responding to it and patients overall are more empowered than 10 years ago."

Plus, in the wake of recalls for drugs like Vioxx, Americans may be more skeptical of what they see advertised, he said.

Kravitz, who has done studies showing higher request rates than Parnes' work demonstrates, remains suspicious of a general drop. He agreed with Parnes that the nature of the ads themselves has changed. There are more ads for extremely expensive drugs like Humira, a medication for rheumatoid arthritis, and for less common conditions, he said. Both could limit requests.

Ads Are Conversation Starters

The new research is not likely to quell calls to ban drug ads. In 2007, Dr. Kurt Stange, the editor of the *Annals of Family Medicine*, declared it "time to ban direct-to-consumer advertising of prescription drugs" because such ads "provide biased educational material and emotional appeals that promote drugs over healthy alternatives."

Of course, those are claims the industry vigorously disputes.

Regulated by the federal Food and Drug Administration, direct-to-consumer advertising "increases people's awareness of disease and available treatments," according to online guidelines from the Pharmaceutical Research and Manufacturers of America [PhRMA], a drugmakers' trade group. Because of the advertising, patients may be more likely to talk to their doctors, PhRMA contends.

"It fosters an informed conversation about health, disease and treatments between patients and their health care practitioners," the guidelines suggest.

7

Low-Income Children Are More Likely to Be Prescribed Psychiatric Drugs

Duff Wilson

Duff Wilson is a staff writer for the New York Times.

Low-income American children who receive health care through the government's Medicaid program are four times more likely to be given powerful antipsychotic medications for mental and behavioral problems than more affluent children who have private health insurance. In addition, they are more likely to be given the drugs for less severe conditions and to be given drugs to treat conditions for which the drugs are not approved. Part of the reason for this disparity is that Medicaid typically pays in full for such drugs but not for counseling or psychotherapy, which can be just as effective, and low-income families are less likely to be able to afford to pursue those options on their own. Some experts think that the stresses of poverty, single-parent homes, poorer schools, and lack of access to preventive health care that many low-income families face may also play a role in shaping the statistics.

New federally financed drug research reveals a stark disparity: children covered by Medicaid are given powerful antipsychotic medicines at a rate four times higher than children whose parents have private insurance. And the Medicaid children are more likely to receive the drugs for less severe conditions than their middle-class counterparts, the data shows.

Those findings, by a team from Rutgers and Columbia, are almost certain to add fuel to a long-running debate. Do too many children from poor families receive powerful psychiatric drugs not because they actually need them—but because it is deemed the most efficient and cost-effective way to control problems that may be handled much differently for middle-class children?

The questions go beyond the psychological impact on Medicaid children, serious as that may be. Antipsychotic drugs can also have severe physical side effects, causing drastic weight gain and metabolic changes resulting in lifelong physical problems.

Children with diagnoses of mental or emotional problems in low-income families are more likely to be given drugs than receive family counseling or psychotherapy.

On Tuesday [December 8, 2009], a pediatric advisory committee to the Food and Drug Administration [F.D.A.] met to discuss the health risks for all children who take antipsychotics. The panel will consider recommending new label warnings for the drugs, which are now used by hundreds of thousands of people under age 18 in this country, counting both Medicaid patients and those with private insurance.

Meanwhile, a group of Medicaid medical directors from 16 states, under a project they call Too Many, Too Much, Too Young, has been experimenting with ways to reduce prescriptions of antipsychotic drugs among Medicaid children.

They plan to publish a report early next year [2010].

The Rutgers-Columbia study will also be published early [in 2010], in the peer-reviewed journal *Health Affairs*. But the findings have already been posted on the Web, setting off discussion among experts who treat and study troubled young people.

Experts Stunned by Disparity

Some experts say they are stunned by the disparity in prescribing patterns. But others say it reinforces previous indications, and their own experience, that children with diagnoses of mental or emotional problems in low-income families are more likely to be given drugs than receive family counseling or psychotherapy.

Part of the reason is insurance reimbursements, as Medicaid often pays much less for counseling and therapy than private insurers do. Part of it may have to do with the challenges that families in poverty may have in consistently attending counseling or therapy sessions, even when such help is available.

"It's easier for patients, and it's easier for docs," said Dr. Derek H. Suite, a psychiatrist in the Bronx whose pediatric cases include children and adolescents covered by Medicaid and who sometimes prescribes antipsychotics. "But the question is, 'What are you prescribing it for?' That's where it gets a little fuzzy."

Too often, Dr. Suite said, he sees young Medicaid patients to whom other doctors have given antipsychotics that the patients do not seem to need. Recently, for example, he met with a 15-year-old girl. She had stopped taking the antipsychotic medication that had been prescribed for her after a single examination, paid for by Medicaid, at a clinic where she received a diagnosis of bipolar disorder.

Why did she stop? Dr. Suite asked. "I can control my moods," the girl said softly.

After evaluating her, Dr. Suite decided she was right. The girl had arguments with her mother and stepfather and some insomnia. But she was a good student and certainly not bipolar, in Dr. Suite's opinion.

"Normal teenager," Dr. Suite said, nodding. "No scrips [prescriptions] for you."

Because there can be long waits to see the psychiatrists accepting Medicaid, it is often a pediatrician or family doctor who prescribes an antipsychotic to a Medicaid patient—whether because the parent wants it or the doctor believes there are few other options.

Though [antipsychotic] drugs are typically cheaper than long-term therapy, they are the single biggest drug expenditure for Medicaid.

Some experts even say Medicaid may provide better care for children than many covered by private insurance because the drugs—which can cost $400 a month—are provided free to patients, and families do not have to worry about the copayments and other insurance restrictions.

"Maybe Medicaid kids are getting better treatment," said Dr. Gabrielle Carlson, a child psychiatrist and professor at the [State University of New York at] Stony Brook School of Medicine. "If it helps keep them in school, maybe it's not so bad."

Medicaid Drug Costs Could Grow

In any case, as Congress works on health care legislation that could expand the nation's Medicaid rolls by 15 million people—a 43 percent increase—the scope of the antipsychotics problem, and the expense, could grow in coming years.

Even though the drugs are typically cheaper than long-term therapy, they are the single biggest drug expenditure for Medicaid, costing the program $7.9 billion in 2006, the most recent year for which the data is available.

The Rutgers-Columbia research, based on millions of Medicaid and private insurance claims, is the most extensive analysis of its type yet on children's antipsychotic drug use. It examined records for children in seven big states—including

New York, Texas and California—selected to be representative of the nation's Medicaid population, for the years 2001 and 2004.

The data indicated that more than 4 percent of patients aged 6 to 17 in Medicaid fee-for-service programs received antipsychotic drugs, compared with less than 1 percent of privately insured children and adolescents. More recent data through 2007 indicates that the disparity has remained, said Stephen Crystal, a Rutgers professor who led the study.

Other Factors May Contribute

Experts generally agree that some characteristics of the Medicaid population may contribute to psychological problems or psychiatric disorders. They include the stresses of poverty, single-parent homes, poorer schools, lack of access to preventive care and the fact that the Medicaid rolls include many adults who are themselves mentally ill.

As a result, studies have found that children in low-income families may have a higher rate of mental health problems—perhaps two to one—compared with children in better-off families. But that still does not explain the four-to-one disparity in prescribing antipsychotics.

Professor Crystal, who is the director of the Center for Pharmacotherapy at Rutgers, says his team's data also indicates that poorer children are more likely to receive antipsychotics for less serious conditions than would typically prompt a prescription for a middle-class child.

But Professor Crystal said he did not have clear evidence to form an opinion on whether or not children on Medicaid were being overtreated.

"Medicaid kids are subject to a lot of stresses that lead to behavior issues which can be hard to distinguish from more serious psychiatric conditions," he said. "It's very hard to pin down."

And yet Dr. Mark Olfson, a psychiatry professor at Columbia and a co-author of the study, said at least one thing was clear: "A lot of these kids are not getting other mental health services."

Medicaid children were more likely than those with private insurance to be given the drugs for off-label uses like A.D.H.D.

Off-Label Uses Common

The F.D.A. has approved antipsychotic drugs for children specifically to treat schizophrenia, autism and bipolar disorder. But they are more frequently prescribed to children for other, less extreme conditions, including attention deficit hyperactivity disorder [A.D.H.D.], aggression, persistent defiance or other so-called conduct disorders—especially when the children are covered by Medicaid, the new study shows.

Although doctors may legally prescribe the drugs for these "off label" uses, there have been no long-term studies of their effects when used for such conditions.

The Rutgers-Columbia study found that Medicaid children were more likely than those with private insurance to be given the drugs for off-label uses like A.D.H.D. and conduct disorders. The privately insured children, in turn, were more likely than their Medicaid counterparts to receive the drugs for F.D.A.-approved uses like bipolar disorder.

Even if parents enrolled in Medicaid may be reluctant to put their children on drugs, some come to rely on them as the only thing that helps.

"They say it's impossible to stop now," Evelyn Torres, 48, of the Bronx, said of her son's use of antipsychotics since he received a diagnosis of bipolar disorder at age 3. Seven years later, the boy is now also afflicted with weight and heart problems. But Ms. Torres credits Medicaid for making the boy's mental and physical conditions manageable. "They're helping with everything," she said.

8

Wichita Witch Hunt— The Justice Department Wages War on Pain Relief

Harvey Silverglate

Harvey Silverglate, author of Three Felonies a Day: How the Feds Target the Innocent, *is a criminal defense and civil liberties attorney in Cambridge, Massachusetts.*

People who have painful chronic conditions have a hard time finding doctors who will prescribe enough medication to help them adequately manage their pain because federal narcotics officers are increasingly arresting and prosecuting doctors—especially those who specialize in pain management—for prescribing too many heavy narcotics to patients. The Drug Enforcement Administration does not seem to understand that patients can develop tolerance to their pain drugs over time so a higher dose may be needed to achieve the same results. Since 2003 more than four hundred doctors have been criminally prosecuted for their pain management prescriptions. In addition, the government has also tried to silence patient advocates who publicly argue for effective pain management. Because physicians are frightened of legal action, Americans who have chronic pain often do not receive enough medication to alleviate their suffering.

No good deed goes unpunished when a private citizen is up against the federal drug warriors—those members of the Department of Justice who have been seeking, with in-

Harvey Silverglate, "Wichita Witch Hunt—The Justice Department Wages War on Pain Relief," Forbes.com, September 1, 2009. Reprinted by Permission of Forbes Media LLC © 2010.

creasing success in recent decades, to effectively control the practice of pain relief medicine. But a current drama being played out in federal court in Kansas portends an even darker turn in the DOJ's war—a private citizen is being threatened with prosecution for seeking to raise public and news media consciousness of the Feds' war against doctors and patients.

The current contretemps in Wichita has its roots in 2002 when Sean Greenwood, who for more than a decade suffered from a rare but debilitating connective tissue disorder, finally found a remedy. William Hurwitz, a Virginia doctor, prescribed the high doses of pain relief medicine necessary for Greenwood to be able to function day-to-day.

Yet when federal agents raided Hurwitz's clinic in 2003 and charged the pain management specialist with illegal drug trafficking, Greenwood's short-lived return to normalcy ended. He couldn't find another doctor willing to treat his pain—the chances were too good that the "narcs" and the federal prosecutors who work with them would assert impossibly vague federal criminal drug laws. Three years later, Greenwood died from a brain hemorrhage, likely brought on by the blood pressure build-up from years of untreated pain.

Greenwood's wife, Siobhan Reynolds, decided to fight back. In 2003 she founded the Pain Relief Network (PRN), a group of activist, doctors and patients who oppose the federal government's tyranny over pain relief specialists.

Now, the PRN's campaign to raise public awareness of pain-doctor prosecutions has made Reynolds herself the target of drug warriors. Prosecutors in Wichita have asked a federal grand jury to decide whether Reynolds engaged in "obstruction of justice" for her role in seeking to create public awareness, and to otherwise assist the defense, in an ongoing prosecution of Kansas pain relief providers. The feds' message is clear. In the pursuit of pain doctors, private citizen-activists—not just physicians—will be targeted.

For Reynolds, the script of the Kansas prosecution has become all too familiar. The feds announced a 34-count indictment at a December 2007 press conference. Local media dutifully reported the charges with minimal scrutiny and the accused—Dr. Stephen Schneider and his wife, Linda, a nurse—were convicted in the court of public opinion before their trial even began.

In such an atmosphere, it is very difficult to make the point that physicians engaged in the good faith practice of medicine are being second-guessed—not by fellow physicians, but by the federal government—and punished under the criminal law for administering what the Drug Enforcement Agency (DEA) of the Department of Justice considers more narcotics than is necessary to alleviate a patient's pain.

When pain doctors administer too much of a controlled substance, or do so knowing that they will be diverted to narcotic addicts, they are deemed no longer engaged in the legitimate practice of medicine. But the dividing line is far from clear and not subject to universal agreement even within the profession. Any patient in need of relief can, over time, develop a chemical dependence on a lawful drug—much like a diabetic becomes dependent on insulin. And, once a treatment regimen begins, many patients' tolerance to the drug increases. Thus, to produce the same analgesic effect, doctors sometimes need to increase the prescribed amount, and that amount varies from person to person.

It is notoriously difficult even for trained physicians to distinguish an addict's abuse from a patient's dependence. Nonetheless, federal narcotics officers have increasingly terrorized physicians, wielding the criminal law and harsh prison terms to punish perceived violators. Since 2003, over 400 doctors have been criminally prosecuted by the federal government, according to the DEA. One result is that chronic pain patients in this country are routinely undermedicated.

The litany of abusive prosecutorial tactics could fill a volume. A "win-at-all-costs" mentality dominates federal prosecutors and drug agents involved in these cases. After a Miami Beach doctor was acquitted of 141 counts of illegally prescribing pain medication in March 2009, federal district court Judge Alan Gold rebuked the prosecution for introducing government informants—former patients of the doctor who were cooperating to avoid their own prosecution—as impartial witnesses at trial.

Improprieties galore marked the prosecution of Dr. Hurwitz. Before his trial in federal court in Virginia in 2004, the DEA published a "Frequently Asked Questions" (FAQ) pamphlet for prescription pain medications. In a remarkable admission, the DEA wrote that confusion over dependence and addiction "can lead to inappropriate targeting of practitioners and patients for investigation and prosecution." Yet on the eve of the trial, the DEA, realizing that Hurwitz could rely on this government-published pamphlet to defend his treatment methods, withdrew the FAQ from its Web site. Winning the case proved more important than facilitating sound medical practice. Hurwitz was convicted.

In Kansas, it appears that zealous prosecutors are targeting not only the doctors, but also their public advocates. When Reynolds wrote op-eds in local newspapers and granted interviews to other media outlets, Assistant U.S. Attorney Tanya Treadway attempted to impose a gag order on her public advocacy. The district judge correctly denied this extraordinary request.

Undeterred, Treadway filed on March 27 a subpoena demanding a broad range of documents and records, obviously hoping to deter the peripatetic pain relief advocate, or even target her for a criminal trial of her own. Just what was Reynolds' suspected criminal activity?

"Obstruction of justice" is the subpoena's listed offense being investigated, but some of the requested records could, in no possible way, prove such a crime. The prosecutor has demanded copies of an ominous-sounding "movie," which, in reality, is a PRN-produced documentary showing the plight of pain physicians. Also requested were records relating to a billboard Reynolds paid to have erected over a busy Wichita highway. It read: "Dr. Schneider never killed anyone." Suddenly, a rather ordinary exercise in free speech and political activism became evidence of an obstruction of justice.

On Sept. 3, a federal judge will decide whether to enforce this subpoena, which Reynolds' lawyers have sought to invalidate on free speech and other grounds. The citizen's liberty to loudly and publicly oppose the drug warriors' long-running reign of terror on the medical profession and its patients should not be in question. Rather, the question should be how the federal government has managed to accumulate the power to punish doctors who, in good faith, are attempting to alleviate excruciating pain in their patients.

9

Mixing Multiple Medications Causes Health Problems for Elderly Americans

Anne Harding

Anne Harding writes about health-related issues for CNN Health.

Because elderly people take so many medications, they are especially susceptible to problems caused by drug interactions. The more medications a person takes, the more risk there is of overmedication and adverse side effects from the drugs interacting with each other. The problem is compounded because the various specialists that seniors often visit usually do not communicate with each other about new medications or dose changes, and they may prescribe new drugs to treat the side effects caused by other ones. Sedatives and hypnotics are among the riskiest drugs for older people because they increase the likelihood of falls and mental confusion, but nondrug therapies can help reduce the use of such medications. Physicians should regularly review the medications of their older patients to be sure they are taking only what is truly necessary.

Many older adults in the United States are taking a confusing combination of medications, some prescribed by doctors and others picked up over-the-counter or in health food stores.

One in three adults age 57 to 85 is taking at least five prescription drugs, and half regularly use dietary supplements and over-the-counter drugs, according to a study in the *Journal of the American Medical Association*. While any single drug might help people live longer, healthier lives, experts worry that a combination of drugs, along with over-the-counter products and dietary supplements, could be a recipe for disaster in terms of drug interactions.

One in 25 people in the study, or about 2.2 million people, were taking a potentially risky combination of medications. That number jumped to one in 10 among men who were 75 to 85 years old.

For example, some people in the study were taking the blood thinner warfarin along with the cholesterol-lowering drug simvastatin, a combination that can increase the risk of bleeding. Others were taking warfarin and aspirin together, or ginkgo supplements with aspirin, which can also cause problems.

Some Interactions Can Be Fatal

"Half of the interactions we saw increased the risk for bleeding, which could be fatal," said Dima M. Qato of the University of Chicago.

An estimated 175,000 adults 65 and older visit the emergency room every year for treatment of adverse drug events, and about a third of these cases involve commonly used medications.

Dr. Stacy Tessler Lindau of the University of Chicago, who led the research team, points out that the 3,005 study participants were on 15,000 different drugs and supplements in all. She says the percentage of people they identified as being at risk of harmful drug interactions is probably an underestimate given that the researchers only looked at the 20 most commonly used prescription drugs, the 20 most frequently used over-the-counter medications, and the 20 most popular dietary supplements.

"I'm hoping that this study encourages patients and families to be proactive about the medications they're using in terms of getting information from their doctors, their nurses, their pharmacists," says Lindau.

Lindau and her team say that "polypharmacy," or the practice of putting people on multiple drugs, is on the rise. A 2002 study suggested that 23 percent of people 65 and older were on five or more prescription drugs at once, compared with 29 percent in the new study.

Lindau and her team interviewed a nationally representative sample of men and women who were 57 to 85 years old between June 2005 and March 2006. They visited participants in their homes and asked to see containers for every drug or supplement they took regularly.

The number of prescription medications an older person takes is the strongest predictor of their risk for future drug-related problems.

"Literally folks went to their medicine cabinet or kitchen cabinet and brought all of the medications to the table," says Lindau.

Prescription Drug Statistics

Eighty-one percent of the study participants were taking at least one prescription drug, 42 percent were on at least one over-the-counter medication, and 49 percent were using one or more dietary supplement

The most commonly used prescription and over-the-counter drugs were for treating or preventing heart disease, such as cholesterol-lowering statins, blood-pressure-lowering drugs, and blood thinners like warfarin and aspirin.

Polypharmacy was most common among the oldest patients, with 37 percent of men and 36 percent of women 75 to

85 years old taking five or more prescription drugs at once. Women were more likely than men to take prescription drugs and dietary supplements.

The number of prescription medications an older person takes is the strongest predictor of their risk for future drug-related problems, says Dr. Donna Fick, an associate professor of nursing and psychiatry at Pennsylvania State University in University Park.

More Medications, More Problems

"Because we know that the more medications you're on the more problems you have, I think we do have to think harder about how to balance medication use with non-pharmacological approaches," says Fick, a specialist in gerontological nursing.

Sedatives and hypnotics are among the riskiest drugs for older people, increasing the likelihood of falls and mental impairment, she pointed out. They are used to reduce agitation in older adults, but research has shown that offering people warm milk, herbal tea and a back-rub can reduce the use of these medications and the likelihood of drug-induced confusion.

Such approaches are "different than this sort of 'fast food' approach to giving a medication, it takes more time and someone has to reimburse for that," Fick notes. "Right now they don't reimburse you to give back rubs and herbal tea, but they do reimburse you to give a medication, and it's faster."

Another problem, she adds, is that there's currently no way for doctors or pharmacists to know every drug, over-the-counter medication and supplement a patient is taking.

Medication Review

People should try to meet with the same doctor every three to six months to go over all the medications and supplements they are taking, Fick recommends. While it's never a good idea to stop taking a prescribed drug without consulting a doctor, she says, "It's reasonable to say 'Do I need to stay on this?'" And it's also reasonable, she adds, to ask about alternatives to medication.

Lindau also suggests that people try to use the same pharmacy whenever possible, so that the pharmacist can catch potential drug interactions.

"That does help maintain the chain of communication," she says. And when buying an over-the-counter drug or supplement, even cold medicine or vitamins, Lindau recommends purchasing it at the pharmacy counter, which can help remind people to ask about safety.

She also suggests that people keep a list of all the drugs and supplements they're taking in their wallet, and make copies to keep by the telephone and to give to family members and friends who might be contacted in case of an emergency.

10

Overuse of Antibiotics Creates Drug-Resistant Bacteria

Martha Mendoza and Margie Mason

Martha Mendoza is an Associated Press (AP) writer who has reported from Norway and England. Margie Mason is an AP medical writer based in Vietnam.

The global overuse of antibiotics has caused bacteria to mutate and become resistant to them. One of the most dangerous is MRSA—Methicillin-Resistant Staphylococcus aureus—*a deadly and hard-to-treat "superbug" that has become common in hospitals everywhere. While hospitals around the world struggle to keep MRSA under control, Norway has all but eliminated MRSA infections by simply not prescribing antibiotics to patients unless they are absolutely essential and by isolating those who do have MRSA until they are well. The result is that the number of MRSA cases in Norway has dropped dramatically; in Norway, MRSA now accounts for just 1 percent of all staph infections, while in Japan it accounts for 80 percent and in the United States 63 percent. Other countries—including the United States—are now adopting Norway's conservative attitude about antibiotics in the hope that it will reverse what the World Health Organization calls one of the world's leading public health threats.*

Aker University Hospital is a dingy place to heal. The floors are streaked and scratched. A light layer of dust coats the blood pressure monitors. A faint stench of urine and bleach wafts from a pile of soiled bedsheets dropped in a corner.

Look closer, however, at a microscopic level, and this place is pristine. There is no sign of a dangerous and contagious staph infection that killed tens of thousands of patients in the most sophisticated hospitals of Europe, North America and Asia this year [2009], soaring virtually unchecked.

The reason: Norwegians stopped taking so many drugs.

Twenty-five years ago, Norwegians were also losing their lives to this bacteri[um]. But Norway's public health system fought back with an aggressive program that made it the most infection-free country in the world. A key part of that program was cutting back severely on the use of antibiotics.

Now a spate of new studies from around the world prove that Norway's model can be replicated with extraordinary success, and public health experts are saying these deaths—19,000 in the U.S. each year alone, more than from AIDS—are unnecessary.

The more antibiotics are consumed, the more resistant bacteria develop.

"It's a very sad situation that in some places so many are dying from this, because we have shown here in Norway that Methicillin-resistant Staphylococcus aureus (MRSA) can be controlled, and with not too much effort," said Jan Hendrik-Binder, Oslo's MRSA medical adviser. "But you have to take it seriously, you have to give it attention, and you must not give up."

The World Health Organization says antibiotic resistance is one of the leading public health threats on the planet. A six-month investigation by The Associated Press found overuse and misuse of medicines has led to mutations in once curable diseases like tuberculosis and malaria, making them harder and in some cases impossible to treat.

Now, in Norway's simple solution, there's a glimmer of hope.

How Norway Found the Answer

Dr. John Birger Haug shuffles down Aker's scuffed corridors, patting the pocket of his baggy white scrubs. "My bible," the infectious disease specialist says, pulling out a little red Antibiotic Guide that details this country's impressive MRSA solution.

It's what's missing from this book—an array of antibiotics—that makes it so remarkable.

"There are times I must show these golden rules to our doctors and tell them they cannot prescribe something, but our patients do not suffer more and our nation, as a result, is mostly infection free," he says.

Norway's model is surprisingly straightforward.

- Norwegian doctors prescribe fewer antibiotics than any other country, so people do not have a chance to develop resistance to them.

- Patients with MRSA are isolated and medical staff who test positive stay at home.

- Doctors track each case of MRSA by its individual strain, interviewing patients about where they've been and who they've been with, testing anyone who has been in contact with them.

Haug unlocks the dispensary, a small room lined with boxes of pills, bottles of syrups and tubes of ointment. What's here? Medicines considered obsolete in many developed countries. What's not? Some of the newest, most expensive antibiotics, which aren't even registered for use in Norway, "because if we have them here, doctors will use them," he says.

He points to an antibiotic. "If I treated someone with an infection in Spain with this penicillin I would probably be thrown in jail," he says, "and rightly so because it's useless there."

Countering Coughs and Colds

Norwegians are sanguine about their coughs and colds, toughing it out through low-grade infections.

"We don't throw antibiotics at every person with a fever. We tell them to hang on, wait and see, and we give them a Tylenol to feel better," says Haug.

Convenience stores in downtown Oslo are stocked with an amazing and colorful array—42 different brands at one downtown 7-Eleven—of soothing, but non-medicated, lozenges, sprays and tablets. All workers are paid on days they, or their children, stay home sick. And drug makers aren't allowed to advertise, reducing patient demands for prescription drugs.

In fact, most marketing here sends the opposite message: "Penicillin is not a cough medicine," says the tissue packet on the desk of Norway's MRSA control director, Dr. Petter Elstrom.

He recognizes his country is "unique in the world and best in the world" when it comes to MRSA. Less than 1 percent of health care providers are positive carriers of MRSA staph.

But Elstrom worries about the bacteria slipping in through other countries. Last year almost every diagnosed case in Norway came from someone who had been abroad.

"So far we've managed to contain it, but if we lose this, it will be a huge problem," he said. "To be very depressing about it, we might in some years be in a situation where MRSA is so endemic that we have to stop doing advanced surgeries, things like organ transplants, if we can't prevent infections. In the worst case scenario we are back to 1913, before we had antibiotics."

The Origins of the Problem

Forty years ago, a new spectrum of antibiotics enchanted public health officials, quickly quelling one infection after another. In wealthier countries that could afford them, patients and providers came to depend on antibiotics. Trouble was, the more antibiotics are consumed, the more resistant bacteria develop.

Norway responded swiftly to initial MRSA outbreaks in the 1980s by cutting antibiotic use. Thus while they got ahead of the infection, the rest of the world fell behind.

In Norway, MRSA has accounted for less than 1 percent of staph infections for years. That compares to 80 percent in Japan, the world leader in MRSA; 44 percent in Israel; and 38 percent in Greece.

In the U.S., cases have soared and MRSA cost $6 billion last year [2008]. Rates have gone up from 2 percent in 1974 to 63 percent in 2004. And in the United Kingdom, they rose from about 2 percent in the early 1990s to about 45 percent, although an aggressive control program is now starting to work.

About 1 percent of people in developed countries carry MRSA on their skin. Usually harmless, the bacteria can be deadly when they enter a body, often through a scratch. MRSA spreads rapidly in hospitals where sick people are more vulnerable, but there have been outbreaks in prisons, gyms, even on beaches. When dormant, the bacteria are easily detected by a quick nasal swab and destroyed by antibiotics.

Do the Right Thing

Dr. John Jernigan at the U.S. Centers for Disease Control and Prevention [CDC] said they incorporate some of Norway's solutions in varying degrees, and his agency "requires hospitals to move the needle, to show improvement, and if they don't show improvement they need to do more."

And if they don't?

"Nobody is accountable to our recommendations," he said, "but I assume hospitals and institutions are interested in doing the right thing."

Dr. Barry Farr, a retired epidemiologist who watched a successful MRSA control program launched 30 years ago at the University of Virginia's hospitals, blamed the CDC for clinging to past beliefs that hand washing is the best way to stop the spread of infections like MRSA. He says it's time to add screening and isolation methods to their controls.

The CDC needs to "eat a little crow and say, 'Yeah, it does work,'" he said. "There's example after example. We don't need another study. We need somebody to just do the right thing."

Exporting Norway's Lessons

But can Norway's program really work elsewhere?

The answer lies in the busy laboratory of an aging little public hospital about 100 miles outside of London. It's here that microbiologist Dr. Lynne Liebowitz got tired of seeing the stunningly low Nordic MRSA rates while facing her own burgeoning cases.

So she turned Queen Elizabeth Hospital in Kings Lynn into a petri dish, asking doctors to almost completely stop using two antibiotics known for provoking MRSA infections.

Around the world, various medical providers have . . . successfully adapted Norway's program with encouraging results.

One month later, the results were in: MRSA rates were tumbling. And they've continued to plummet. Five years ago [in 2004], the hospital had 47 MRSA bloodstream infections. This year they've had one.

"I was shocked, shocked," says Liebowitz, bouncing onto her toes and grinning as colleagues nearby drip blood onto slides and peer through microscopes in the hospital laboratory.

When word spread of her success, Liebowitz's phone began to ring. So far she has replicated her experiment at four other hospitals, all with the same dramatic results.

"It's really very upsetting that some patients are dying from infections which could be prevented," she says. "It's wrong."

Around the world, various medical providers have also successfully adapted Norway's program with encouraging results. A medical center in Billings, Mont., cut MRSA infections by 89 percent by increasing screening, isolating patients and making all staff—not just doctors—responsible for increasing hygiene.

In Japan, with its cutting-edge technology and modern hospitals, about 17,000 people die from MRSA every year.

Dr. Satoshi Hori, chief infection control doctor at Juntendo University Hospital in Tokyo, says doctors overprescribe antibiotics because they are given financial incentives to push drugs on patients.

Hori now limits antibiotics only to patients who really need them and screens and isolates high-risk patients. So far his hospital has cut the number of MRSA cases by two-thirds.

VA Hospitals See Success

In 2001, the CDC approached a Veterans Affairs [VA] hospital in Pittsburgh about conducting a small test program. It started in one unit, and within four years, the entire hospital was screening everyone who came through the door for MRSA. The result: an 80 percent decrease in MRSA infections. The program has now been expanded to all 153 VA hospitals, resulting in a 50 percent drop in MRSA bloodstream infections, said Dr. Robert Muder, chief of infectious diseases at the VA Pittsburgh Healthcare System.

"It's kind of a no-brainer," he said. "You save people pain, you save people the work of taking care of them, you save money, you save lives and you can export what you learn to other hospital-acquired infections."

Pittsburgh's program has prompted all other major hospital-acquired infections to plummet as well, saving roughly $1 million a year.

"So, how do you pay for it?" Muder asked. "Well, we just don't pay for MRSA infections, that's all."

A Mother's Crusade

Beth Reimer of Batavia, Ill., became an advocate for MRSA precautions after her 5-week-old daughter Madeline caught a cold that took a fatal turn. One day her beautiful baby had the sniffles. The next?

"She wasn't breathing. She was limp," the mother recalled. "Something was terribly wrong."

MRSA had invaded her little lungs. The antibiotics were useless. Maddie struggled to breathe, swallow, survive, for two weeks.

"For me to sit and watch Madeline pass away from such an aggressive form of something, to watch her fight for her little life—it was too much," Reimer said.

Since Madeline's death, Reimer has become outspoken about the need for better precautions, pushing for methods successfully used in Norway. She's stunned, she said, that anyone disputes the need for change.

"Why are they fighting for this not to take place?" she said.

11

"Doctor Shopping" Can Lead to Overmedication, Abuse, and Death

Madison Park

Madison Park is a writer and producer for CNN Health.

Michael Jackson, Anna Nicole Smith, Health Ledger, Corey Haim. What all these big-name celebrities have in common—besides dying tragically—is that they are believed to have been "doctor shoppers" who obtained numerous prescriptions for powerful painkillers and sedatives by visiting a variety of different physicians under false pretenses. The abuse of prescription medications is a growing problem, and doctor shopping is one of the primary ways that prescription pill addicts get their drugs. Most states do not require physicians to check a patient's drug history, and doctors say it can be very difficult to tell who comes to them with a legitimate need and who just wants to obtain drugs. Prescription monitoring programs and increased drug abuse screening in clinics and doctor's offices are two ways to combat this problem.

Former child actor Corey Haim had prescriptions for as many as 553 dangerous drugs in the last year of his life, and it's the result of "doctor shopping," California's top law official said [in April 2010].

The issue of doctor shopping—visiting numerous doctors to fraudulently get prescription drugs—has been raised in numerous celebrity deaths, including Anna Nicole Smith, Michael Jackson and Heath Ledger. Doctors say they often rely on their own instant judgments in the office and have little reliable means of double-checking the patients' information.

"It puts doctors in the uncomfortable position of playing private eye," said Dr. Lance Longo, medical director of Addiction Psychiatry at Aurora Behavioral Health Services in Milwaukee, Wisconsin. "We're trained to relieve pain and suffering. Unfortunately, with the widespread misuse of controlled substances and diversion risks, we're often taken advantage of."

Haim obtained doses of Vicodin, Valium, Soma, Oxycontin and Xanax from seven doctors, filled at seven pharmacies, said California Attorney General Jerry Brown in a news conference [in April 2010]. Vicodin and Oxycontin are painkillers; Valium and Xanax are anti-anxiety medications; Soma is a muscle relaxant.

The 38-year-old actor died last month [March 2010] after collapsing at a Los Angeles apartment. . . .

Haim had visited several emergency rooms and urgent care clinics with complaints of an injured shoulder or depression, according to investigators.

Doctor Shoppers Dupe Doctors

Doctor shoppers often visit facilities where medical professionals don't know them, experts say. They also call during weekends or ask for prescription refills using excuses such as having dropped the pills in toilets or getting pills wet on a camping trip, physicians said.

Misuse of prescription drugs is a growing problem. Estimated hospitalizations for poisoning by prescription opioids, sedatives and tranquilizers increased 65 percent from 1999 to 2006, according to a study in the May [2010] edition of the *American Journal of Preventive Medicine*.

Doctor shopping is a problem, but it's not the chief way prescription drugs end up with people for whom they're not intended, said David Brushwood, professor of pharmaceutical outcomes and policy at the University of Florida in Gainesville.

"It's a relatively insignificant source of diverted prescription drugs, as compared with theft from drug stores, warehouses, acquisition over the Internet, theft from people's homes."

To curb prescription drug abuse, 34 states have prescription monitoring programs, but their requirements and effectiveness vary, experts said.

In those states, a record from the prescription drug purchase is sent to the state agency that oversees the monitoring programs. Doctors can request reports online and find out what medications a patient has received in the past six months to a year.

This information helps doctors, said John Eadie, director of the Prescription Drug Monitoring Program Center of Excellence at Brandeis University.

"There are doctor shoppers, who see 15 doctors and pharmacies or more by deceiving physicians for professed pain and other disability that would cause prescribing these drugs," he said. "If doctors know they are obtaining drugs from other prescribers, they might be really reluctant to prescribe."

But these monitoring programs have limitations, Brushwood said.

It's easy to dodge the system by providing different names and identification numbers or buying drugs in neighboring states, he said. Most state laws do not require the doctors to look at the patient's drug history.

Many health professionals don't use the monitoring system anyway, Brushwood said. In his research, many expressed skepticism about the accuracy of the information and complained it was "time consuming" and did not "seem necessary," he said.

Screening Can Identify Likely Addicts

Doctors have other tools to prevent being duped.

"We're doing addiction screening in our clinics," said Dr. Doris K. Cope, professor and vice chairman for pain medicine in the department of anesthesiology at the University of Pittsburgh School of Medicine. "If someone is at high risk for addiction, we try to identify them, and we have one of our pain psychologists evaluate them. We then make appropriate referrals for their continued care."

"This is the addiction epidemic of our time."

They also test urine to see whether it matches the patient's medication history.

"If someone comes in and can barely move, they put on this big drama, then you see them get up and run out the door, even my youngest son could figure that out," said Cope, a member of the American Society of Anesthesiologists' Committee on Pain Medicines.

Some employ clever strategies such as memorizing symptoms to get a certain prescription or telling their doctors they have allergies to particular medication to get a stronger drug. But physicians have to walk a fine line, said Longo, a psychiatrist.

"We all have the expectation to practice prudent, conscientious medicine, but we're not trained to be DEA [Drug Enforcement Administration] agents," Longo said. "We don't want to alienate patients who aren't addicted or abusing drugs. The majority of patients who have legitimate illnesses feel stigmatized getting controlled drugs."

Some of the popularly abused drugs include oxycodone, hydrocodone, benzodiazepine and methamphetamine.

"This is the addiction epidemic of our time," Longo said.

Organizations to Contact

The editors have compiled the following list of organizations concerned with the issues debated in this book. The descriptions are derived from materials provided by the organizations. All have publications or information available for interested readers. The list was compiled on the date of publication of the present volume; the information provided here may change. Readers need to remember that many organizations take several weeks or longer to respond to inquiries.

Alliance for the Prudent Use of Antibiotics (APUA)
5 Kneeland St., Boston, MA   02111
(617) 636-0966 • fax: (617) 636-3999
e-mail: apua@tufts.edu
website: www.tufts.edu/med/apua

Alliance for the Prudent Use of Antibiotics's mission is to strengthen society's defenses against infectious disease by promoting appropriate antimicrobial access and use, and by controlling antimicrobial resistance on a worldwide basis. Its website offers extensive information for consumers and doctors about the proper use of antibiotics and the danger that their overuse will lead to their ineffectiveness.

Center for Drug Evaluation and Research
Food and Drug Administration, Silver Spring, MD   20993
(301) 796-3400
e-mail: druginfo@fda.hhs.gov
website: www.fda.gov/cder

The Center for Drug Evaluation and Research promotes and protects the health of Americans by assuring that prescription and over-the-counter drugs are safe and effective. The center routinely monitors TV, radio, and print advertisements to see that they are truthful and balanced. It publishes the *News Along the Pike* newsletter as well as various reports.

Center for Public Integrity

910 Seventeenth St. NW, Ste. 700, Washington, DC   20006
(202) 466-1300
website: www.publicintegrity.org/rx

The Center for Public Integrity is a nonprofit, nonpartisan, nonadvocacy, independent journalism organization. Its mission is to produce original investigative journalism about significant public issues to make institutional power more transparent and accountable. It conducts a project titled Pushing Prescriptions: How the Drug Industry Sells Its Agenda at Your Expense, which has a website with extensive information about the political influence of the pharmaceutical industry.

Children and Adults Against Drugging America (CHAADA)

e-mail: info@chaada.org
website: www.chaada.org

Children and Adults Against Drugging America is a membership organization whose goal is to raise awareness about what it perceives as the overmedicating of America and the deception occurring within the psychiatric profession—which it views as preying on innocent people, especially children, in order to turn a profit—and the dangers of the drugs used to treat alleged mental illnesses. The organization opposes the use of all psychotropic drugs. Its website contains extensive material about personal experiences with the adverse effects of drugs and about drug-related legislation.

International Coalition for Drug Awareness

website: www.drugawareness.org

This organization is a private nonprofit group of physicians, researchers, journalists, and concerned citizens focused on "the world's most pervasive and subtle drug problem—prescription drugs." Available at its website is the full-length film *Prescription for Disaster*, an in-depth investigation into the symbiotic relationships between the pharmaceutical industry, the FDA, lobbyists, lawmakers, medical schools, and researchers. The site also includes material about individuals' negative experiences with prescription drugs and links to many sites about specific drug dangers.

International Federation of Pharmaceutical Manufacturers and Associations (IFPMA)

15 Chemin Louis-Dunant, Geneva 20   1211
  Switzerland
e-mail: admin@ifpma.org
website: www.ifpma.org

International Federation of Pharmaceutical Manufacturers and Associations is a nonprofit, nongovernmental organization representing pharmaceutical industry associations from both developed and developing countries. It aims to encourage a global policy environment that is conducive to innovation in medicine, both therapeutic and preventive, for the benefit of patients around the world. Its website contains information about its position on issues such as improving access to health care, the ethical promotion of drugs, and the problem of counterfeit medicines.

National Council on Patient Information and Education (NCPIE)

200-A Monroe St., Ste. 212, Rockville, MD   20850-4448
(301) 340-3940 • fax: (301) 340-3944
e-mail: ncpie@ncpie.info
website: www.talkaboutrx.org

National Council on Patient Information and Education is a coalition of over 125 diverse organizations whose mission is to stimulate and improve communication of information on appropriate medicine use to consumers and health-care professionals. NCPIE publishes educational resources, including *Make Notes & Take Notes to Avoid Medication Errors*. Its website contains a section designed to help caregivers and patients become well-informed medicine users who know where to go for reliable information, and what questions to ask.

National Pharmaceutical Council (NPC)
1894 Preston White Dr., Reston, VA   20191
(703) 620-6390 • fax: (703) 476-0904
website: http://npcnow.org

Supported by more than twenty of the nation's major research-based pharmaceutical companies, National Pharmaceutical Council sponsors research and education projects aimed at demonstrating the appropriate use of medicines to improve health outcomes. It focuses on the use of evidence-based medicine to help patients make the best, most cost-effective healthcare decisions. Monographs on disease management, newsletters, and other publications geared to policy makers, healthcare providers, employers, and consumers are available on its website.

No Free Lunch
e-mail: contact@nofreelunch.org
website: www.nofreelunch.org

No Free Lunch is a nonprofit organization of health-care providers and medical students who believe that pharmaceutical promotion should not guide clinical practice. Its website has slide presentations on the relationship between physicians and the pharmaceutical industry as well as information for patients, including a directory of doctors who have pledged not to accept gifts from drug companies.

**Pharmaceutical Research and Manufacturers
of America (PhRMA)**
950 F St. NW, Ste. 300, Washington, DC   20004
(202) 835-3400 • fax: (202) 835-3414
website: www.phrma.org

Pharmaceutical Research and Manufacturers of America represents US drug research and biotechnology companies. It advocates public policies that encourage discovery of important medicines, and its medical officers sometimes testify before

Congress on issues such as drug advertising, safety, and importation. Among its publications is *PhRMA Guiding Principles: Direct to Consumer Advertisements About Prescription Medicines.*

PharmedOut

Georgetown University, Washington, DC   20057
(202) 687-1191 • fax: (202) 687-7407
website: www.pharmedout.org

PharmedOut is an independent, publicly funded project that empowers physicians to identify and counter inappropriate pharmaceutical promotion practices. Its website offers many links to YouTube videos, articles, and Web resources that are of interest to consumers as well as doctors.

Worst Pills, Best Pills

Public Citizen, Washington, DC   20009
website: www.worstpills.org

Worstpills.org is researched, written, and maintained by Public Citizen's Health Research Group, a division of Public Citizen, which is a nonprofit, nonpartisan public-interest group that represents consumer interests in federal government at all levels: Congress, the executive branch, and the courts. Although most of its information about specific drugs is accessible only to subscribers, its website contains a number of free consumer guides, including "Misprescribing and Overprescribing of Drugs," and "Drugs, Money and Politics," among others.

Bibliography

Books

John Abramson	*Overdosed America: The Broken Promise of American Medicine.* New York: HarperPerennial, 2008.
Marcia Angell	*The Truth About the Drug Companies.* New York: Random House, 2005.
Peter R. Breggin and Dick Scruggs	*Talking Back to Ritalin: What Doctors Aren't Telling You About Stimulants and ADHD.* Rev. ed. Cambridge, MA: Da Capo Press, 2001.
Greg Critser	*Generation Rx: How Prescription Drugs Are Altering American Lives, Minds, and Bodies.* Boston: Houghton Mifflin Harcourt, 2005.
Lawrence Diller	*Running on Ritalin: A Physician Reflects on Children, Society, and Performance in a Pill.* New York: Bantam, 1999.
Ray Moynihan and Alan Cassels	*Selling Sickness: How the World's Biggest Pharmaceutical Companies Are Turning Us All into Patients.* New York: Nation Books, 2006.
Ray Strand and Donna K. Wallace	*Death by Prescription: The Shocking Truth Behind an Overmedicated Nation.* Nashville: Thomas Nelson, 2003.

Judith Warner | *We've Got Issues: Children and Parents in the Age of Medication*. New York: Riverhead Books, 2010.

Ethan Watters | *Crazy Like Us: The Globalization of the American Psyche*. Glencoe, IL: Free Press, 2010.

Marilyn Webb | *The Good Death: The New American Search to Reshape the End of Life*. New York: Bantam, 1999.

Periodicals

Alliance for the Prudent Use of Antibiotics | "Shadow Epidemic: The Growing Menace of Drug Resistance," Executive Summary of the 2005 GAARD Report. Boston: APUA, 2005.

Karen O. Anderson et al. | "Racial and Ethnic Disparities in Pain: Causes and Consequences of Unequal Care," *Journal of Pain*, December 2009.

Associated Press | "Haim Got Pills Via 'Doctor Shopping'—Actor Reportedly Got 553 in His Final Two Months," *San Diego Union Tribune*, April 7, 2010.

Douglas J. Edwards | "Report Raises Concerns About Overmedicating Seniors," *NH News Notes: Nursing Homes*, August 2003.

Judy Holland   "Are Kids Being Overmedicated?—Psychiatrists Say Schools Steer Parents to Overmedicate Kids," *New York Times*, October 2, 2000.

Gregory M. Lamb   "Why Are We Taking So Many Pills? Marketers Have Convinced Many That There's a Drug for Everything," *Christian Science Monitor*, October 25, 2005.

Elizabeth Large   "Americans Are Taking More Prescription Drugs than Ever Before, Raising the Question: Are We an Overmedicated Society?" *Baltimore Sun*, December 17, 2004.

Jonah Lehrer   "Depression's Upside," *New York Times Magazine*, February 25, 2010.

Catherine Lewis   "Why Is Your Doctor Getting Your Child Hooked on Unnecessary Drugs?" *Insiders Health*, November 9, 2009.

Rick Mayes and Jennifer Erkulwater   "Medicating Kids: Pediatric Mental Health Policy and the Tipping Point for ADHD and Stimulants," *Journal of Policy History*, vol. 20, no. 3, 2008.

Elizabeth J. Roberts   "A Rush to Medicate Young Minds," *Washington Post*, October 8, 2006.

Vera Sharav   "America's Overmedicated Children," *Youth and Medicines*, June 1, 2005.

Maia Szalavitz	"Let a Thousand Licensed Poppies Bloom," *New York Times*, July 13, 2005.
Time	"Are We Giving Kids Too Many Drugs?" November 3, 2003.
Barry Yeoman	"Prisoners of Pain—Why Are Millions of Suffering Americans Being Denied the Prescription Drug Relief They Need?" *AARP Magazine*, September & October 2005.

Index